T0367196

The Condition of Secrecy

ALSO BY INGER CHRISTENSEN

Inger Christensen

The Condition of Secrecy

selected essays

translated by Susanna Nied

 A NEW DIRECTIONS PAPERBOOK ORIGINAL

DANISH ARTS FOUNDATION

The Condition of Secrecy was published with the assistance of a translation subvention
from the Danish Arts Foundation.

Excerpts from: Elias Canetti, *The Torch in My Ear*, tr. Joachim Neugroschel (Farrar, Straus
& Giroux); Inger Christensen, *The Painted Room*, tr. Denise Newman (Harvill); Leonardo
da Vinci, *The Notebooks of Leonardo da Vinci, Vol. 1*, ed. and tr. Jean-Paul Richter (Dover
Publications); Gunnar Ekelöf, *En röst: efterlämnade dikter och anteckningar* (Albert Bonniers
Förlag); Benoit Mandelbrot, *The Fractal Geometry of Nature* (W. H. Freeman & Co.); Maurice
Merleau-Ponty, *The Merleau-Ponty Reader*, ed. Ted Toadvine & Leonard Lawlor (North-
western Univ. Press); Jacques Monod, *Chance and Necessity*, tr. Austryn Wainhouse (Alfred A.
Knopf); Novalis, *The Novices of Sais*, tr. Ralph Manheim (Curt Valentin); Novalis, *Philosophical
Writings*, ed. and tr. Margaret Stoljar (SUNY Press).

William Blake, *Newton* (p. 104), copyright © 2018 by Tate, London.

The poster on p. 138 was photographed by Anders Sune Berg.

First published as a New Directions Paperbook Original (NDP1430) in 2018
Manufactured in the United States of America
New Directions Books are printed on acid-free paper
Design by Erik Rieselbach

Library of Congress Cataloging-in-Publication Data
Names: Christensen, Inger, 1935–2009 author. | Nied, Susanna, translator.
Title: The condition of secrecy : essays / Inger Christensen ; translated by Susanna Nied.
Other titles: Hemmelighedstilstanden. English
Description: New York : New Directions, 2018. | Includes bibliographical references and index.
Identifiers: LCCN 2018021516 (print) | LCCN 2018025539 (ebook) | ISBN 9780811228121 (ebook) |
ISBN 9780811228114 (alk. paper)
Classification: LCC PT8176.13.H727 (ebook) | LCC PT8176.13.H727 H4613 2018 (print) |
DDC 839.814/74—dc23
LC record available at https://lccn.loc.gov/2018021516

10 9 8 7 6 5 4 3

New Directions Books are published for James Laughlin
by New Directions Publishing Corporation
80 Eighth Avenue, New York 10011

Contents

The Condition of Secrecy

Freedom, Equality, and Fraternity
in the Summer Cottage

Where are you going for summer vacation?" Today, we're likely to answer with place names that give off a powerful warmth of their own, names of "true" summer lands by the Mediterranean. But back then—between 1939 and '49—we were usually going either "no place" or maybe "over to the summer cottage." The first answer meant that we'd stay home in Vejle, where we lived in an ordinary apartment on an ordinary street; the other meant that when my father's vacation came up, we'd move a little way out of town, to the south side of Vejle Fjord near Munkebjerg, where the Tailors' Union owned a cottage.

It was at home or in "The Tailors' House" that the word *summer* gained meaning for me and grew full of the experiences that I've later used to top up all other summers to extra fullness: summer as a morass of luxuriance. Yet at that time I tended to see it as having a lack of experiences—especially during a summer when we didn't go "over to the summer cottage."

The reason we said "over to the summer cottage" instead of "out to the summer cottage" must have had to do with its placement on a high hill—actually tremendously high, when we had to push our loaded bicycles up—but on the other hand it provided the satisfaction of being called "Blaze Mountain," a name that gave off the powerful warmth of a true summer land.

And that warmth is probably the most powerful summer experience, the feeling of warmth filling your body so completely that there's no difference, no perceptible boundary, between the air and your skin. When it gets to that point, someone always says, "Today it's summer," with extra emphasis on "-day," meaning both "Summer is finally here" and "Tomorrow it will all be over." You sink down into a chair or the grass, in either shade or sun, with that sudden and afterward enduring feeling of warmth throughout your body—the scent and the heat blended in a relationship that lends immediacy, or the possibility of immediacy, to all hot, muggy, sultry, scorching, etc. experiences.

In the same way there's a whole string of glimpses, images, moments of awareness, when summer became apparent and instilled itself in us: the path behind the gasworks, where black pieces of coke crunched underfoot and where there was always a multitude of yellow slugs on the sunny side, moving like slow flames—that was on the way out to the garden by the cove, where the earth got so dry it cracked, and where we were always making finds because there had once been a trash dump; sometimes the earth was so hard and gray-white that you could scratch it like the shards of porcelain we found—or that evening when, wending our way back to the cottage, we learned the phrase *still as glass*. Or that evening ... or that evening. Today it's summer, we'd say then. Black coke, porcelain, and a sea shining like glass.

But in that string of warm summer images, some experiences stand out especially. I'm thinking of three: a wide meadow deep with the pink wildflowers called "lady's smocks," a noontime that I spent bouncing my big beach ball against the glowing wall of the house, and a night when a thunderstorm came up, and we gathered in the kitchen and ate strawberries.

They're three banal experiences, nothing out of the ordinary; many people must have seen and done the same things, but for me they stand out. They were for many years almost supernatural, are still nearly indescribable, and I know by now that I have to let them stay beyond words, because they're about a child's—a human being's—in this case, my own—first aesthetic experiences. Even back when they first happened, these three images were already what I can now call them: three images—open, endless beauty; pointless energy; and the security of not being alone.

If we could just go "over to the summer cottage," then summer was saved. Then we had a real summer land to conquer. And we had a house. Although it belonged to us only because it belonged to others, I don't think that mattered much to us—maybe we preferred to ignore it—and over the long term, it worked its way in and became, to say it dramatically, an image of freedom, equality, and fraternity. The solidarity of the union members' volunteer work on the house and yard on Sundays was striking because it was so unremarkable— at least to us children, it seemed unremarkable, something we never thought about; it was simply all of us working together, pruning trees, making steps out of railroad ties, picking apples, painting garden furniture, spreading gravel, lowering the little pier into the water, having coffee and snacks, playing ball, raising the flag, singing, and swinging in the swing hung from the August apple tree. Now, much later, I know there were some members who didn't participate, and I'm sure there was some muttering about them. That's part of the adult world. (Besides, this must have been wartime, but we didn't notice the war during the summer; it belonged to the basement back on our street at home, where rows of benches were set up in an underground shelter, it was basically only there that we belonged to the war, especially at night, especially during winter; it was absolutely a winter experience; even if we were home all summer, we didn't notice the war. During the summer, we forgot so fast.)

It seemed unremarkable that we belonged to that group of union members, where the old tailors sat around on Sundays talking about the days when they barely got a Sunday free from work. The fear of that kind of endless work week made us worry that something might threaten the house—and especially the apple trees, before the apples got ripe. But the two very old, thin, white-haired tailors who were the best storytellers always laughed so loudly when they talked about the old days that we almost thought it was something they'd made up, and not a true account that had elements of the exotic slavery described in children's books.

In that way Sundays became an experience of the fact that there were families other than ours, whom we didn't know, but with whom we were in a community. (Of course nobody said that; that's not the kind of thing people talked about.) And it might have seemed like all we were doing was drinking coffee and chatting and gossiping and eating picnic lunches—but beneath the surface, there was that image of summer: we're not alone.

Every spring, my brother and I would start pestering to go "over to the summer cottage," not only on Sundays and on especially warm, clear summer evenings, but also for our father's whole vacation. And every year, I think my mother thought it was too much trouble. It certainly was, for the adults: feather comforters, clothes, food, everything had to be bundled up and tied onto the bicycles, and with those enormous loads, which could be almost as tall as my father who rode in front, we pedaled along the narrow, twisting, rutted, and incredibly hilly forest path, in and out along the fjord, until we labored our way up the last steep hill and triumphantly took possession of the cottage.

Then for eight or fourteen days we would live not in an ordinary apartment, but in a house, with gardens, a forest, and a view out over the fjord. We had a bedroom with a balcony and a basin and pitcher, and we drank our morning coffee on a terrace with its own nest of swallows. There was a plate rack in the living room, a window seat, colored panes of glass, and white-painted furniture—all things we didn't have at home—a fancy stove in the kitchen, and a deep, cold cellar with bottles of beer and Star brand soda. And there was the room with hangers and a mirror where the women changed into their bathing suits. And there was the shed with the chopping block, and the blue plums that never managed to get ripe.

The house itself was half-timbered, with a tarred foundation, and way down at the bottom of the broom-covered hillside lay the railroad track. We could see every train that ran between Vejle and Fredericia—between us and the rest of the world—and not one escaped having its cars counted, and being waved at, and listened to long beforehand and long afterward—we maintained that they kept us awake at night.

The yellowness and blackness, the tar, the railroad ties and broom, the dangerous train and the blinking signal lights, the sun and the dizziness when we lay out for too long, these all stretched summer out and kept it in motion, as much as the black coke and yellow slugs behind the gasworks.

And without really realizing it, we also experienced anxiety at the core of summer, when we were out picking wild blueberries or blackberries and our father and mother disappeared into the depths of the thicket where there were poisonous snakes. But we did have our rubber boots on and we were heroic, and we nourished high ambitions of picking the most berries of all.

For it wasn't an anxiety that overwhelmed or overshadowed other things. It was a natural kind of anxiety; it had the same lightness and the same weight as joy; it was part of an interplay where first one, then the other was more apparent, a light uneasiness, as the wind turned the fronds of bracken so that all their black spore eyes stared out.

Or my brother and I would lie on our bellies down on the pier, watching crawdads and fish and flickers of sunlight, and waiting for our father and mother, who had gone into town for groceries, watching for them in every tiny dot that moved along the curving coastline, guessing whether that might be them, and when it finally was, exploding into such a fast run that our whole bodies became outbursts of emotion, as dogs' bodies do.

Summer was warmth and many other good things, and thunder and poisonous snakes and many other forms of excitement. And of fear. Early on, mine focused on a turkey who was my first deadly enemy, and from whom I was rescued by a dog named Bitsy. Next it focused, more silently and deeply, I think, on a statue that was—at least at the time—huge. It stood in front of our nearest neighbor, the summer cottage of the "navers," carpenters who traveled from town to town, literal journeymen. Once I was lifted up to shake the statue's tar-hot, outstretched hand; I looked into the giant face under the broad-brimmed black hat and was terrified. I don't remember specifically, but I'm sure I thought that he was alive. But I do know that I thought these beings in their odd, traditional garb, the navers (the word sounded like "knaves" or "gnawers"), were some kind of underground creature, like trolls or unusually large dwarves. And when they sat around their warped picnic table, drinking and roaring "Skaal!" and we all had to walk past, I was afraid for the tailors. They couldn't possibly be a match for giant statues.

Of course I later learned that it was fun to shake hands with that stiff, peaceable traveling tradesman with the kindly outstretched, painted hand of stone—especially in daylight, it was fun. But when I think back on it—and I almost always sit on the side of the train where I can see him, when we go past—I know that I had to transform him into an image of something that threatened, every year, to prevent us from "going over to the summer cottage."

He had taken up a position at the entrance to our true summer land. We had to get past him, and we had no chance against him. Normal human anxiety, which a person encountered every day and understood, that was part of summer. But this stone colossus belonged to a different world—a world beyond the realm of aesthetic experience.

(1966)

Interplay

When I was nine years old, the world, too, was nine years old. At least there was no difference between us, no opposition, no distance. We just tumbled around from sunrise to sunset, body and earth as alike as two pennies. And there was never a harsh word between us, for the simple reason that there were no words at all; we never uttered a word to each other, the world and I. Our relationship was beyond language—and thus also beyond time. We were one big space (which was, of course, a very small space).

And right at that point in time (where there were no points in time) our school began teaching us about all the world's points in time. We started studying world history. We'd looked hugely forward to this step up, and especially to getting away from our dull, slow-paced Danish history class; it had been trying our patience for quite a while, and besides, Denmark was no longer big enough for us; in fact, nothing was big enough for us. We—meaning thirty more or less advanced schoolgirls—always wore dresses made of *plaid* rayon, which always had to be lengthened in a *single* color— anyone could see that the dresses had never been intended to look like that—and thus that it had never been intended for us to look like that either. We were growing at an absolutely wild pace—not only in height, but in the most obvious other dimensions as well, and there just seemed not to be enough room for us, because we had only that one space to move around in.

Yet even a world history class couldn't change anything about our intimate relationship with that space. We were still one, and those breasts beginning to bud were just a kind of outcropping in the vast whole, a kind of upthrust in the earth's crust, which did activate our sensors but never became a major catastrophe. It wasn't time yet. For it turned out that our world history class had nothing at all to do with time. The only thing that happened was that we all got crushes on our world history teacher, and that the Sparta he evoked became part of our crushes. We did our very best to have our passion reciprocated; we went so far as to identify completely with that iron-hard Spartan boy. Even if we couldn't transform him into a man, at least we could turn him into a god. We worshipped proudly and obediently, dutifully doing the exercises he laid out and following the precepts he set forth in our autograph books:

> *Be brief, clear, and firm*
> *And let your thoughts be known.*
> *Stand by what you say*
> *And keep your mind your own.*

If our space, our world, hadn't acquired time, it had certainly acquired depth. And it had definitely been stirred up. Even though the world was still only nine years old, it was full of giddiness, asceticism, and incomprehensible dreams.

When I turned ten, the world suddenly turned ten million billion years old. How it happened, or when it happened, I don't know. Maybe it was the night when I first looked through a telescope. Though that would be almost too easy, and most of all it would be almost too perfect, to be able to say that time entered into one's life in that way. But who knows. And what does "time entered into" mean? How does a person experience that? In any event, it didn't have to do with suddenly noticing that I was ten years old. When I was ten, I didn't notice being ten. Just as now, at thirty-five, I barely notice that I'm thirty-five, although occasionally I do suddenly notice that I'm acting as if I were just ten, actually that I am ten and childish curious naive awkward and full of laughter. But back then, at the time, I didn't notice that. What I noticed wasn't about being ten years old or being young at all; it was about being older: it was as if my body suddenly, on its own, from one day to the next, had started practicing for something I hadn't the faintest inkling of, as if there were some twenty-, twenty-five-, or thirty-year-old body practicing something inside me, making me move in new and strange ways, even making some of my cells notice themselves: grown up determined all-knowing confident and tragic.

It was, to put it briefly, as if my cells had been divided into two types, as if a membrane had been lowered between "me" and "my space", and the cells on one side could see the cells on the other side. Could press up against them, so that pressure and counterpressure arose. Osmosis was needed, and so it began.

Like a battle between an anonymous body and an official person (between a body in space, in nature, and a person in time, in culture).

Like an exchange between a space that gradually became captivity, and a time that could gradually become freedom.

What had previously been a neutral relationship was suddenly transformed into a weighted interplay.

Interplay: between being simultaneously captive and free. The first time I experienced that was May 4, 1945, when I was ten years old and heard a loudspeaker announce that World War II had ended, or more accurately that Denmark had been liberated. My heart pounded, and at the same time I felt embarrassment. But *embarrassment* is too strong a word. Or too early a word. More accurately, what happened was that my heart pounded and the other parts of my body were immediately mobilized to bring my heart and body into equilibrium again. As if my heart, which at once had been attracted toward the world and toward freedom, was quickly reminded of its place, certainly in that same world, but as a captive.

So now it's not too early to say that I felt embarrassment. It's always embarrassing to be a captive. So embarrassing that we stealthily turn it around, so it almost looks like we are embarrassed about being free. Motions that are too big and too sentimental are used to cover up the embarrassment. Later we're embarrassed about the sentimental motions. And so on. We remain captive, exactly when we are most free.

That May 4 went on to include a rite that made my heart pound again, even more powerfully and for more diverse reasons. The church held a service of thanksgiving, where I stood among a thousand other children and belted out "O Great King of Kings, You Alone Can" so loudly that Jesus, floating there on the frescoed wall with his rainbow, had to be able to hear and ultimately free me to come up between the goats—which he gently pushed behind him into the alcove arch with one hand, as if he were sending them to stand in a corner, a captivity—and the sheep, which with the other lightly outstretched hand he beckoned through space toward light and freedom. There I stood with my pounding heart, maintaining my righteousness. But at the same time I knew how shameful it was to put myself first like that, even if only in a flash of thought, so I hurried, stealthy as I apparently was by nature, into a flash of a different thought that included simultaneously the prayer I was singing to high heaven. In a very primitive way an individual experience had led to something not individual—in this interplay that's built into human beings, one that, when a person dares to sidestep it, forces that person to return to it, even if she doesn't know why she's doing so and even if she always comes up with other, more primitive reasons for doing so. For instance, she can think she's afraid of her own pridefulness. But why is she afraid? Why is it inappropriate to pray for our own sake alone, to pray not to land among the goats? It's because by doing so, we are betraying the substance we are made of, the substance we have in common with the world and thus with other people. But *betraying* is already saying too much. The word *betraying* implies that it's possible to betray. As if there were a difference between what we're made of and how we act. There is not. The physical world and the inner world are one, indivisible. Our physical interplay with each other is a reality. So our inner interplay is also a reality. The body and the inner self, the inner image, follow the same inexplicable principles. And our only consolation for the lack of an explanation is that we share an inability to explain it. It's our intersubjective will, our collective psyche or psychosis, our shared captivity. It's within this captivity that our shared freedom must be sought.

So there's also no reason to cultivate individual experience, individual psychology. It's a fiction, because it suggests that there's a kind of freedom beyond the purely physical freedom that we own only in our interplay with the world and with each other. For that reason I consider it more important to posit an incorrect explanation of the world than to present an explanation of an individual self that may well be correct. And more important to posit the reality of the *image* than to refer to the existence of the body. More important to further conscious control over that invisible interplay than to cultivate conscious control over a fictive entity, the individual.

The second time I experienced the interplay between freedom and captivity, it was on a more commonly discussed and definitely no less physical plane. It was the springtime when I started to notice myself as I ran. When I realized that I was no longer running just to run; I was also running to be seen as someone who ran, who could run faster than anyone else on the block (because the boys were growing so slowly), and who would never, under any circumstances, start running like those young wives with their odd, coquettish gait who zigzagged up the street at five minutes to noon because they'd forgotten to buy salt for the potatoes. The springtime when I suddenly discovered that my heart would pound, that I would get a stitch in my side and taste blood in my mouth, and that of course I was running to the finish, but not only to run; also to be caught. By a boy.

Here for the first time I experienced the triumph of freedom within captivity. As if the mortal humiliation of being caught were transformed from the inside and became the highest honor. Captivity and freedom were part of each other. And they knew it. Because a perfect interplay existed between the two states of consciousness in that little scene. Posit: that this interplay exists among us all.

(1970)

The Dream of a City

Dreams are like poems and other ways of interacting: before we know it, they've dug their way in and brought forth a string of particularly enduring clichés. If you've ever dreamed, as Freud says we all must, then you can do it again and again, and if you've ever seen something repeat itself, then you can see it again and again—and pretty soon you don't see anything else: Poetic Customs and Practices #64, a ghost in full armor.

It's with that kind of tangible windmill that a writer does battle when he critiques his work and thus his life. A few years ago the Swedish writer and critic Göran Palm said something like this: "Why write about horses, when we know that most farmers have tractors?" Many writers, both before and since that came up, have changed their approaches after that kind of response. In today's poetry there are numerous chromed elements gleaming with the same light as the shining horses of the past—it's only natural. But why not carry the question to its logical extreme, ride a bit further out, and shift poetic strategies: why write about nature at all, when most people live in cities?

If I may: that, of course, is nonsense. And: there is, of course, something in it worth discussing.

A couple of years ago I was living in Knebel, down by Mols. My window had a view of trees, a field, and sky. I carried on long conversations with that view, and I continued them when I went for walks in the countryside, where there was always some far-flung comment to find along the beach, up in the hills, or among the clusters of houses and farms. A conversation that had been carried on for centuries, one that I more or less patiently continued weaving—almost as patiently as the farmer with his plow, regardless of whether he was using a horse or a tractor. One day he said, "The rewards aren't worth the effort; it'd be better to live in town." This classic reason for flight from country to city suited me perfectly; I packed up my pen and paper and left. And though it wasn't exactly that simple, today I think it's simple enough; no other explanation fits any better.

Ironically, now that I live in Copenhagen I have the same view I had before: trees, a field, and sky. But for many reasons the conversations we carry on are far from the same. For me there's one overarching reason: so many people.

A statement like that might be interpreted as a terse and provincial expression marveling at a metropolis and all its inhabitants, a cliché dragged out of some secretary of tourism's suitcase and slightly revised, a dream of heady action and sweet lives in abundance.

But not all dreams are clichés. In any case, more than once, at irregular intervals, I've had a dream that can't be packed into my private cliché case, at least not yet. It just won't shrink enough. Over time, its theme and main features have become increasingly specific and clear; only the details change. It may begin with me walking into a tiled bathroom with all sorts of fixtures. That doesn't surprise me, even though I had no intention of walking into it. With utter trust, I then see that it's no longer a bathroom; it's now a bakery, a dairy, a butcher shop, or a public swimming pool, and as the rooms freely change, and I walk on through long corridors with decorative ponds, through offices and royal chambers with smoky glass, through parlors to hallways to rooms with government officials, to communal kitchens, through trolley cars, etc., I understand that I've come into a city, the only way a person can come into it: from inside. And when I finally stand looking out over the square or the park, and then stroll across the green lawns, I feel perfectly happy. Not so much because of the city itself, but because of the infinite number of people who, wherever I go, are in the middle of some task or other, and who are also in the middle of tasks there in the park. Some of them I recognize from other places and times in my life; others— possibly most of them—I don't; but still, without amazement, I find it perfectly natural that there's no difference in my relationship to the known people and the unknown ones. That's what makes me happy. Only one thing bothers me: that I can't talk with all these people. But I reassure myself that it's because they exist only in my consciousness. Then I wake up.

Of course one of those cities is a dream, the other a reality—or are they? In the real world, too, it's clear to me that my consciousness has become like a city, and that the rewards of my move to this new work environment are, so far, more than worth the effort. From a reasonable degree of manageability, with a more or less fixed number of possibilities for encounters, and an accordingly calm pulse rate, I've now settled myself in a place where the feeling of unmanageability is impossible to ignore, where my consciousness is detached from my environment, and above all, where anonymity is a fact of life.

I want to live as centrally as possible in this anonymity. I'd like to live in the town hall square, in keeping with the image of a city as a view to hold a conversation with. I often peacefully nurture fantasies about a city nearly the size of Denmark. In brief: I want to feel that I live in the mass society I really do live in. And it's that unmanageable and anonymous mass society that I'm referring to now, when I say that a writer has a duty to seek out a work environment.

Naturally, there are good reasons for fearing anonymity. It means that the individual is vulnerable, lonely, and in the long run superfluous—there are so many other people anyway. And if we turn for a minute to the dynamics that all these people set in motion in our societies, then the anonymity almost does induce fear: unforeseen production leads to new unforseen production, on and on, with a blind hope that the multitude of byproducts will be useful. A powerful experience of this anonymity and of the apparently sovereign acceleration of this social mechanism can easily give rise to the well-known feeling of "everyone for himself." And when the first steps are taken in that direction, then there is a real danger that mass society will move toward mass annihilation, either physical or psychological.

But another mass society, with exactly the same conditions, can do the opposite: it can invite us to take part in aspects of humanity that we haven't known about; it can awaken our curiosity, our urge to see what is actually going on. And really: isn't this an excellent work environment for a writer? Politicians put their best efforts into coordinating and finding connections between what has happened and what is going to happen. I believe that's a job that must be tackled on many different fronts; and without being either overly ambitious or overly modest I feel that writers represent one of those fronts. The concept of living in a city—an environment not having what we usually think of as an "environment," without borders, with a feeling that supports that social order—that concept is what I want to see used as a foundation for critiquing writers' work.

I think that too much weight is laid on self-realization. I think that, as a counterweight to the unmanageability of the world, a cult of the individual springs up, maybe even of the unmanageability of the individual—as an attempt to create balance, but on a shaky foundation. If we writers can't work things out by any other means, we can always stake out a single area, act as if we're documenting it, and thus provisionally legitimize the structures of this false environment. Or we can stake out strangeness, crawl down into cellar doors and through sewer systems, turn our souls inside out or hide in attics.

Maybe it can't be any other way. But I'm not so sure.

Jens Ørnsbo, in the most recent issue of *Vindrosen*, writes, "Increasingly, literature in peaceable societies has to live on more or less inflated crises or situations of conflict." He adds, "This last problem, a lack of problems, is becoming apparent."

I don't believe that.

Can writers write only if they're provoked by crises, conflicts, and problems? And if so, how about using the following problem: what is it, actually, that we're taking part in? What is a mass society? What is this city: a work of art, a mobile, a set of building blocks—or what? It must be possible to write our way into these questions.

The day we can put mass society into the cliché case will be the day we've found a new name for it. We dream, despite everything, of a more human way of expressing what we are now living.

(1964)

To Talk, To See, To Do

WHAT WE DON'T TALK ABOUT

There are a few, very few, things worth talking about—and we don't talk about them. We can't talk about them. For instance life, death, and love. We give them big, expensive names, something like a dress so good that we're not comfortable wearing it. We're shy. We're afraid. So we don't mention it. That kind of word is left hanging in the closet, while we use all the nice, ordinary, and undeniably practical words in our daily dealings with each other.

We're afraid. But we manage. We're afraid to be alone and afraid to be with others; afraid of what's finished, at a standstill, too orderly; and afraid of what's unfinished, messy, and disorderly—and we're afraid of sex, afraid of death. But we manage. Or do we? Could it be that the reason we're still having wars is that we're afraid to tell each other that we're afraid of each other, and of everything else? To me it's as if we keep going out in the rain—and keep refusing to invent raincoats and galoshes.

WHAT WE DON'T SEE

We don't talk about the things we don't know anything about, the things we can't do anything about, the things we can't see. But those are the things that fascinate us. If a person seems attractive, ultimately it's not because of this or that external feature; it's because

20

of the internal interplay among those features. And that interplay is invisible. We'd like to be able to guess one another's thoughts, put ourselves in one another's place—you just can't tell what's going on in people's minds, we say. All we know is that there's something else, something more than what we see.

This recalls a Baroque anecdote (related by Saint-Simon): One winter a set of wax masks had been made to look like all the people of the court. At a ball the wax masks were worn under other, ordinary ball masks, and when the ordinary masks were taken off, everyone was fooled and thought they were standing with the real person, but they were really standing with a wax mask of one of the other people there. Underneath, there was someone entirely different. Everyone was greatly amused by this joke.

WHAT WE DON'T DO

Underneath, there's someone entirely different. That's certainly worth talking about: how to get this other, fearful, helpless person out, so he's no longer so afraid of being helpless that he has to wage wars to battle his own fear. One of Gunnar Ekelöf's notations:

> I have, in imagination, lived through all the shamelessness and corruptibility of which the first half of the twentieth century consists. I have also, at a much earlier age, seen people pale, in shock, along Unter den Linden, and during that same year I saw battlefields with not a house left standing, not a tree. That was in 1920. And then the war in Spain. And then World War II, Korea, Vietnam, and racism on all fronts, lust for power on all fronts. I want to serve.... But I will never forget what I have seen, and I think about it constantly. How shall human beings be good. At times I think that human beings are evil animals; at times I think I glimpse a solution, perhaps when I'm in a woman's arms.

I see no other solution for humanity than an underground one ... the secret meal, underground opposition to all forms of oppression ...

Someone has said: we must change ourselves, if the world is to be changed. That is not a Christian thought; it's heathen. That's the way I see it.

That's pretty much the way I see it, too. The individual must change himself. Must show that underneath, there's someone entirely different.

WHAT WE DO ANYWAY

I have, in my imagination, lived ...", says Ekelöf. In imagination. That is, in words. He said that he was afraid, and he told us that at last he was no longer afraid of being afraid, because he had figured out that he wasn't anyone special and had accepted it—"in reality, you are no one"—and he found a kind of comfort in that. The important thing is that he had the courage to keep telling it to others, to say it again and again: I'm afraid. I'm no one. Isn't that the way it is for you too? ... How else can we put aside the lust for power in all of us?

WHAT WE SEE ANYWAY

Of course we can see perfectly well that that's the way it is. We just don't like to face it. And if we finally do face it, we close our eyes tightly afterward, so it can't slip out and disturb us anymore. We think we've put a truth in its place so firmly that it neither will, nor can, move again. But there is no truth. There's only a movement toward ... no, not toward a truth, maybe toward a better humanness, a better life with each other. Many people tell themselves that poetry is certainly one thing that has to tell the truth (or at least to tell *some* truths). But poetry is not truth. It's not even the dream of truth; poetry is passion—it's a game, maybe a tragic game, one that we play with a world that plays its own game with us.

WHAT WE TALK ABOUT ANYWAY

An old Chinese anecdote about pure passion:

> The master said to his followers: "I need someone to carry a message to Hsi-t'ang. Who will take it to him?"
> Wu-feng said, "I will."
> "How will you get the message to him?"
> "When I see Hsi-t'ang, I'll tell it to him."
> "What will you say?"
> "When I come back, I'll tell you."

Through this writing, I've been trying to get to the heart of my relationship with my readers.

I want them to talk about what they don't talk about. What we talk to ourselves about anyway, deep inside.

I want them to see what they don't see. What we see all the time anyway, but are afraid to put into words.

I want them to do what they don't do. What we want to do anyway, if we ever could become helpless enough to do it.

(1969)

Our Story About the World

Nature has its necessity, its direction, its force.

A flower can't suddenly stop and decide not to bloom.

A child can't have second thoughts about being born and stay inside its warm mother.

And the earth can't change its route and head out for a trip around Jupiter, or out beyond the solar system.

But what about art?

Is there anything called art's necessity, its direction and force?

Does art originate from the same necessity that gives rise to beehives, the songs of larks, and the dances of cranes?

Is it a natural expression that unavoidably bursts forth as an extension of what already exists? A natural phenomenon like all others, something that sets itself in motion, necessitated by the forces of nature, occasionally using a human being as its workplace?

And is it just as vital for human beings, as necessary for maintaining life, as the hive is for bees, the song is for larks, and the dance is for cranes?

Granted, it's hard to call Michelangelo a workplace.

But if we say that art expresses itself through him, he's not diminished, just as he isn't diminished when we say that he expresses himself through art. Surely both are happening.

And in that single, indivisible, unified expression, both Michelangelo and art itself are in connection with what is puzzling and mysterious about the necessity of natural phenomena.

It's true that everything is chance and change, but only because there also is an order.

Only because simultaneously, beneath what is changing and inexpressible, there is an order and a beauty that can burst forth at any time.

Because even though we may never swim in the same river twice, it's still the river called Ganges, Mississippi, or Po that we're swimming in.

All that flowing changeability, borne up by what is eternally the same. Michelangelo as a ripple on the surface of art.

One could say that it's not the individual works of art that are necessary, but art per se.

As the earliest humans spoke, we speak too, and our speech, without our noticing how it happens, can lapse into rhythm, become a song or a poem, so that getting up in the morning, for instance, can become a song of joy about getting up.

And in the same way, all our normal ways of moving can suddenly become dance.

In the sounds of the tools we use, we suddenly hear music, which we pursue and continue as we go on with our work, or instead of going on with our work.

And because our senses are always in play, our household items acquire decorative touches, our fabrics acquire colors and designs. Our children receive toys and our dead receive gifts, and it all seems essential.

For just as the wind can draw patterns in water and sand, and rustle in leaves, and whistle in chimneys, and blow the clouds around so that they dance and die, so Michelangelo can also draw and paint and whistle at the same time, and see swirling visions of what hasn't yet been created.

The question is whether humans are at all able to avoid building boats, once they've seen a floating branch and their bodies have felt that it can bear their weight.

Whether we are at all able to do without art, once it has lifted us into a context, no matter how light and temporary, which gives us a glimpse of the unbroken wholeness of the universe.

25

Certainly we can drink water from a faucet, just as it is. But once we've seen water spurting from the mouth of a sculpted lion or fish, or streaming from the mouths of dragons, swans, or gods, then we thirst for water from those works of art, no matter how much regular tap water we drink.

Not for the sake of entertainment. But because works of art can be experienced as pieces of our story about the world, in which we tell each other, in pictures, words, shapes, figures, that the world has an overarching meaning, even though it is hidden.

A meaning that's not always dependent on whether we can see what the individual parts of the story are supposed to represent. Because meaning can emerge just as clearly, maybe more clearly, without any directly representational elements, as in music or abstract art.

Although artistic movements away from representational realism have not been without their problems.

For example, when the visual arts began moving toward abstract depictions of motion—the motion that permeates reality itself.

And stopped depicting things, but instead depicted the relationships that matter for things. The breakdowns and shifts that create or fail to create harmony.

Also by highlighting the pure, unbridled joy of trying to grasp the shared life of color and form.

"Anyone at all could have painted that," people say. "A chimp could have painted that." "My kid could have painted that." "Heck, I could have painted that myself, if I'd wanted to."

And that is both true and completely untrue.

No matter what, the fact that all of us can paint, and think we can paint, and generally can reach preliminary agreement about it, is an expression of the necessity of art.

That's why it must be considered remarkable that artists have been able to paint exactly what anyone else could have painted.

This "anyone else," whether chimps or children or anyone at all, also includes the artist. And what the artist has always already expressed. Michelangelo too. Also when he paints what no one else at all could have painted.

What I'm getting at here is the connections and differences among all entities on earth.

Our abilities, development, and understanding as a shared project.

Stones and insects, rainforests, humans, and cloud formations, all as a collective necessity.

If we couldn't sing, play instruments, and dance, if we couldn't tell stories and describe the world for each other, we would never be able to understand the world, nor would the world ever be able to understand itself through us.

All the knowledge we have is, in a certain sense, already gathered in the great works of art.

For that reason it's also impossible to imagine intellectual or scientific creativity that doesn't draw on forgotten childhood experiences, on experiences of nature, literature, music, etc.—of everything that has brought us wonder, everything we remember without knowing we remember it, everything that makes us wish and hope, everything we love, or worship, or feel ourselves part of. But also everything we hate. Including our hatred of the fact that we can destroy, and we can die. And kill.

In the second volume of his memoirs, *The Torch in My Ear*, Elias Canetti describes how day after day in Frankfurt, he sought out Rembrandt's painting *The Blinding of Samson*, in order to learn about himself. The painting shows two soldiers gouging out Samson's eyes, while Delilah, who hired the soldiers, exults in the background.

"I often stood in front of this painting, and from it I learned what hatred is. I had felt hatred when very young, much too young, at five, when I had tried to kill Laurica with an ax. But you don't know what you have felt: you have to see it in front of you, in others, in order to recognize it and know it. Something you recognize and know becomes *real* only if you have experienced it previously. It lies dormant in you, and you can't name it; then all at once, it is there, as a painting, and something happening to others creates itself in you as a memory: now, it is real."

When we write poetry, the process can often start in contemplation of language.

And it's exactly that concentration on words and combinations of words, which, in themselves, are essentially empty, that can elicit key memories.

Memories that will make it possible for readers to access their own memories.

In this way we come to live in a shared linguistic process, where experience and the creation of art are interwoven.

Just the fact that I can both see and be seen. And that I can see myself. And see myself see. See myself being seen. Also by others. Who themselves see and are seen. This already comprises the seed of art's necessity.

"Is this waterfall of images really a house?"

That's a quote from one of my own poetry volumes, *Letter in April*, but it was originally a comment made by my son—six years old at the time—as we watched a TV program about the architecture of India.

The program featured the temple of Shiva in Madurai, the camera slowly panning over the whole vast wealth of figures adorning the outer walls. "Is this waterfall of images really a house?"

Yes, it is. One needs only to have experienced a waterfall. Or to know what it is. To know that there is something called images. And one needs to be able to see the images as a coursing stream, as opposed to the static thing one previously thought of as a house.

And this image-stream of a house, which belongs to consciousness, could easily be called beehive, lark-song, and crane-dance.

For as human beings, we can't avoid being part of the artistic process, where source, creation, and effect are inextricably bound together.

Here in our necessity.

(1989)

Silk, the Universe, Language, the Heart

Silk is a noun. All nouns are very lonely. They're like crystals, each enclosing its own little piece of our knowledge about the world. But examine them thoroughly, in all their degrees of transparency, and sooner or later they'll reveal their knowledge. Say the word *silk*, and it vanishes with the sound, but your senses, your memory and knowledge cast back an echo. Write it on a piece of paper, and it stays there, unmoving, but your thoughts and feelings are already on their way to the farthest corners of the world. That's what I mean about the loneliness of nouns; each one has to be self-contained, as if it were the only word that existed. As if *silk* were the only word, and is therefore able at any time to awaken our encapsuled knowledge not only of silk, but of the world itself. Even of forgetting. Just try to forget the word *silk*, and you'll be reminded of it next time you see the summer sky, a flower petal, or the membrane between two muscles in a butchered chicken.

I found *silk* in the writings of Lu Chi, in his Ars Poetica. He was born in China in 261 A.D. and executed, age forty-two, in 303 A.D. Like his father and grandfather, he held a high military rank, but he was summarily executed after a violent battle by the Yangtze River, when he lost so many soldiers that their corpses blocked the river's flow. For ten years of his short life he lived in seclusion, immersed in studies. He left behind three hundred poems and essays, among them a little book about the art of writing, where I found *silk*.

"In a single meter of silk, the infinite universe exists." That's what Lu Chi writes. He writes the Chinese word for silk, paints the word with his brush, as he must have done so often, on a piece of silk. I think I can see him sitting there, his brush dipped in ink but still only partly lifted, listening within himself, while the only thing visible to his inward-turned gaze is the silk, the emptiness and boundlessness, the infinite universe, from which he pulls in his perspective at the moment that he lifts the brush and writes the word *silk*.

Maybe the silk was blue. All adjectives are very helpless. They never really have much substance. Day after day, they have to cling to all the nouns they can find. So *blue* always has to cling to the sky, to the iris of the eye, to chicory, bluebells, and copper sulfate, to the reflection of the sky in lakes and seas. It would be the same if the silk were white. Then *white* would have had to cling to snow and rice, to lilies and pearls and cooked fish, to stars and teeth. And now the silk, white or blue, with the help of these helpless adjectives has already become able to leave its aloneness as a noun, and is on its way toward snow or the sky, chicory or the pearl, and farther on into the infinite. Or else the infinite is on its way into the silk. Maybe I should say the *apparently* infinite. Or does the infinite already encompass that, the apparently infinite? For instance, the longest silk thread in the world could never be called *apparently infinite* if the concept of infinity didn't already exist.

Lu Chi must have known that, because he had known silk all his life. His family was very well off and owned large rice fields and mulberry groves near the Yangtze delta, and bamboo groves in the hill country by Lake Hangzhou. Of course Lu Chi could easily have written the word *silk* on silk without thinking of the silk moth; but often enough he probably thought of it, and maybe especially of its larva, the silkworm, which lives on mulberry leaves, and of its silken web, where it pupates in a small cocoon. The outer part is densely matted, the inner part almost parchment-like, the middle part best of all for silk production, but it turns out to be one continuous silk thread approximately four thousand meters long. So maybe Lu Chi never could write the word *silk* without thinking of the four thousand meters of thread inside every single cocoon. Summer after summer, he saw silkworms by the thousands in the mulberry groves, transforming their small bites of mulberry leaves into cloaks of apparently infinite silk thread. Apparently infinite, or infinite? Maybe Lu Chi just told himself that the apparently infinite is what looks like infinity, if infinity could be seen. Or maybe he thought that infinity not only encompasses the apparently infinite, but that in its infinite nature, it is also encompassed by its own apparency, so that at the moment when the silk thread was shuttling back and forth across the loom, Lu Chi truly was able to see infinity woven into its every single meter.

But maybe Lu Chi didn't use adverbs at all. The parts of speech that we call adverbs may not even exist in Chinese. I could look it up. But ultimately it's beside the point here. I should simply avoid adverbs. As far as possible. But adverbs are quite strong-willed. And fairly insistent. They always find a way in. Like *apparently*, for example. It absolutely had to position itself before the adjective *infinite*. Regrettably, when with no problem at all it could have put itself in front of so many other adjectives. Apparently alone, apparently helpless, apparently motionless. But right is right. It does seem that the space in front of *infinite* is glaringly empty, and there aren't very many adverbs that want to position themselves there. Not *quite* infinite, or *rather* infinite, or *very* infinite. Not even *insanely* or just *unusually*. Maybe *constantly*. But *apparently* got there first. Apparently infinite. And like all other adverbs, it wants to take control, weigh values, pronounce judgments. So that nouns and adjectives can barely manage to be alone together and move about on their own. Just look at the quote from Lu Chi. Adverbs would have ruined everything: "In a single meter of silk the apparently infinite universe exists." That's not how silk should be treated. Especially not by a person like Lu Chi, who trusts his own and others' capacity to conceptualize.

If we think we can cast the shadow of logical questions over Lu Chi's silk sentence, if we flatly think that what he writes about silk and the universe is wrong, or if we reduce it to a so-called poetic metaphor, then we haven't understood Lu Chi. According to Lu Chi, logical questions have nothing to do with poetry. The language of poetry is infinite, but the language of logic is only apparently infinite. All in all, language is pre-logical, while logic is a specialty with a limited range, a very useful specialty that lets us speak objectively about what we call an objective world. But it is also a very dangerous specialty, because we clearly have a tendency to confuse this objective world with the world itself. Yet Lu Chi doesn't let himself be fooled into making language less than the reality it's connected to. Language can't be separated from the world without separating the world from itself. That's why Lu Chi answers, even before these predictable questions are asked, by presenting his silk clause in conjunction with another, about language: "In a single meter of silk, the infinite universe exists; language is a Great Flood from a small corner of the heart." Silk, the universe, language, and the heart—he links them by creating two parallel clauses that flow into each other and unite only when they have reached far beyond our field of vision.

Lu Chi's whole book consists for the most part of these parallel structures, in two-line stanzas that rhyme, but that don't function as formal couplets, because each individual line is irregular, as in prose poems. This specific form is called *fu* in Chinese. Earlier, the *fu* form was used for long narrative poems about historical events or for praise poems to royals and other leaders. But Lu Chi renovated the *fu* form by using it in his Ars Poetica. In fact, the word makes up half the title of his book: *Wen Fu*. It's not an outwardly prepossessing book. Around thirty pages, with twenty-one sections whose concise titles highlight what matters most when poets work with words. The sections deal with simple but very complex things like how to begin and how to choose words, or with harmony, originality, fear, inspiration, or how to find a form. Lu Chi even presents a direct overview of existing forms, calling one section simply "Catalog of Genres." Despite this single-minded concentration on the practice of writing, there are also silk, the universe, language, and the heart in numerous sections, woven together in a living pattern. A pattern that is ceaselessly created and transformed, as things arise consecutively with words. So the world, which once came into being on its own, and which, via human beings, let words come into being, now comes into further being in the poem, in an awareness of itself, of its own origin and its ongoing existence.

All verbs are very agreeable. They come into being on their own whenever there's movement. They move and let themselves be moved. They keep everything in motion, including themselves. They shift, change identity, and undo every noun's loneliness for a while. They're always wandering around, and they're always thrusting themselves forward to ask, investigate, and specify things, and to come up with new possibilities. So all verbs are very open and multiply very easily. In countless variations, they express the verb *to be*, although a few verbs do keep more or less completely to themselves. For example, *shall, can, must,* and *will* keep to themselves, outside verbs' normal interchangeability. They function as constant markers of sorts, occasionally stepping in to give other verbs a push in the right direction. But on the whole, verbs fluctuate so much that one is tempted to say the whole course of language is the course of verbs. It's due in large part to verbs that language becomes a Great Flood, a story that deluges everything. This total deluge that from a small corner of the heart becomes language—this silk that contains the infinite universe, this ceaseless streaming back and forth between consciousness and vision—is unthinkable without the energy of verbs, united in the verb *to be*. Which makes it possible simultaneously to differentiate and to not differentiate between what *is* in what. Language is in the heart, which is in language. The universe is in silk, which is in the universe.

In *Wen Fu*, Lu Chi tries to grasp this mysterious miracle play as the natural phenomenon that it is. Significantly, he tries to grasp it by using the word *wen*. In Chinese, *wen* is one of the oldest words of all, at least three thousand years old. Even that far back, when people were casting oracle bones onto black stones so they could shine into the universe as letters, *wen* meant "art," in the form of either literature or sculpture. Etymologically, at its most basic, *wen* simply means "design" or "structure," a structure where meaning and form are so indissolubly bound together that one is inconceivable without the other—no form without meaning, and no meaning without form. This is why *wen*, also meaning "to write," is the most natural way to express the deepest part of consciousness, the center, expressed in a Chinese character that blends "heart" and "mind." So Lu Chi's use of the word *wen* gains a multitude of meanings. It's only on the surface that it means "literature"; in reality, it also means "responsibility," including a responsibility to tell the truth, which can be defined along the lines of calling things by their true names.

If we call things by their true names, that doesn't mean that the names are being used to represent things, and it doesn't mean that language mimics reality as a thing that is separate from language. Rather, a kind of threshold condition arises, where language and the world express themselves with the help of each other. The world, with its natural extension in language, comes to a consciousness of itself, and language, with its background in the world, becomes a world in itself, one steadily unfolding further. That's why it can be said that by writing poetry, we're trying to produce something that we ourselves are already a product of. The heart, which from its own small corner overflows with all sorts of random occurrences gathered with the help of a lifetime of heartbeats, perhaps trying to recognize an order in it all before it stops beating—and silk, which, in its interwoven synthesis of nature and culture, plays with an empty space so utterly newly created and full of possibility that it can take in the universe and encompass it, working it in on itself like a Möbius strip and letting it stay in that unfathomable flux between outside and inside. These concepts and their relationship (silk, the universe, language, and the heart) would be impossible for us to talk about if all we could use were nouns, adjectives, adverbs, and verbs. Or more accurately, our use of all these very lonely, helpless, strong-willed, and agreeable words would be impossible if they weren't anchored in all the comparisons and relationships that the world consists of, discreetly expressed by nearly invisible prepositions, which we can best love by using them as precisely as possible.

All prepositions are nearly invisible. They bear language up in the same way that outer space bears planets up. In their limited numbers, *up, down, out, in, over, under,* etc. keep our consciousness in the same kind of motion that the world is in. They place all nouns in relationship to each other and mutely assure us that we're borne up in advance in the world by an inexhaustibly huge, ever-present foundation of comparisons. At one time I immersed myself in the work of Danish linguistics expert Viggo Brøndal, who wrote, among other things, a book called *A Theory of Prepositions.* There he tries to systematize prepositions to reflect the idea that the relationships they refer to in language are already in place in the world giving rise to language. So he divides the relationships into categories with names like symmetry, transitivity, continuity, connectivity, variability, extension, integrity, and universality, arranged in a taxonomy of increasing complexity. In the concluding section, on universality, he writes, "The most wide-ranging synthesis would ultimately encompass all zones and degrees of relationship: abstract, concrete, and complex; primary and secondary; central and peripheral. That kind of total relationship must, in keeping with its nature, exist at the boundaries of thought; as an expression of the quality of experience, it must be of an almost mystical character."

What is the source of this mystical character? Maybe it's that the forms already exist in the world. A tree exists in its tree-configuration, and so my life too, or my whole family's lives, can take on that configuration. But not as a resemblance; more nearly as a form that's the same. And one that could also be the form of a poem. And here, forms must be considered not as static, but as ongoing processes, occasionally made clear, also in an interplay with our sensory systems. When forms are considered in that way, more similarities than differences emerge in a comparison of cells' chemical workings to support the body as a form, and words' workings to support the world as a poem. The word has, in principle, the same chemistry that's needed to set the process of crystallization in motion. Seen from outside, in their random states—for instance in a dictionary—words look like chaos. But fundamentally they're always in order, at home, so to speak, with their phenomena. Meanwhile we're thinking that it's up to us to organize the words into sentences and oppositions before everything can be put in order. Nothing could be more inaccurate. The order we're trying to organize our way into already exists. The opposition we set up between chaos and order is of our own making. We invent a certain way of looking at things, a way that we think keeps things in order, but without understanding that this way of seeing is itself a kind of order. It's in this labyrinth of consciousness and the world intertwined that we find ourselves, where no one can know which comes first, the world or consciousness. The French poet Bernard Noël has an excellent description of poets' situation in this context: "We write in order to get to the last word, but the act of writing constantly delays that. In reality, the last word can be anywhere at all in what we write. Or maybe it's everything we write. In that way, when I write, I'm chasing a shadow—and it's my chasing it that keeps the shadow in motion."

This is how we must view silk, the universe, language, and the heart. They're parts of the shadow that we're chasing. Shadows of silk, of the universe, of language, and of the heart; and as we chase them, they merge with each other and even with the shadow of god. Or as Lu Chi didn't write, but might well have written: Things vanish into the shadows of each other and of themselves; but with the reflections of those shadows, poems return to light.

(1992)

The Condition of Secrecy

What we sense when we read a poem is the motions of the mind. Not only the poet's mind, and not only our own, but both, intermingled in the poem, as if the poem were our minds' common ground.

As we read, we may feel that language is far too light, but if the poem is good, then even the heaviest subjects will be hidden in that lightness; maybe because each individual word is so packed with energy that it contains millions of ways to experience things.

The same millions of ways to experience things can be used when we write a poem. Everything is contained in everything.

But only if the poem is what we call beautiful does it contain all those possible ways to experience things; a poem that's too ordinary contains nothing greater than the poet's own way of experiencing things; and that can definitely be very ordinary.

If the poem is good, the words have so much energy that the heaviest subjects can seem almost weightless; if the poem is bad, it not only weighs down everything the reader tries to bring to it; it also weighs itself down.

There's no sure way to determine whether a poem will be beautiful or banal, good or bad. The best we can do in practice is not only to read quantities of poems written by others, but also to truly read our own poems—that is, to read them while we're writing them, and continuously revise them, until at last they reflect some kind of light, some kind of insight, as if they had been written by others, by someone else.

It may not be so hard to recognize a good poem once it's there. But how can we find our way to it before it's there?

How can we get vague thoughts and impressions to combine with the reality that will evoke them, so that not only the thoughts, but also the reality itself will be expressed? And how can we get form and content to live and grow with and within each other, as plants, for example, grow in the natural world?

This is all something that we can study and read and write theory books about, and that's all useful, but only the kind of usefulness that has to sink completely into oblivion before it can show what it's useful for. Because writing poems, no matter what, is always about being at square one and starting from scratch; every time, about writing the individual poem as if it were the first poem in the world.

But only *as if* it were the first. The best thing, though impossible, would be to be able to read and remember all the poems that have ever been written, in order to forget them at the decisive moment. To forget them in the same way that we, as children in school, learned handwriting, and suddenly one day forgot about making the specified motions with our hands and pencils and could just write, on our own, spontaneously. A small and mysterious miracle, when one thinks about it.

Writing poems is just as much a mysterious miracle. Not that there's anything mystical or ceremonial about it. Or anything religious. It's a neutral miracle, so to speak, granted in advance, because in the process of writing we need to use language in its whole, indissoluble connection with reality. It's that connection that's a mysterious miracle And that's what poetry has to enter into.

Unlike our logical-practical language, poetry can't ignore parts of reality and, under conditions that we've set in advance, act as if it were humanly possible to tell the truth about the world.

Maybe poetry can't tell any truths at all. But it can *be* true, because the reality that accompanies the words is true. This secret-filled correlation between language and reality is how poetry becomes insight. A mysterious miracle that may well be the condition of secrecy Novalis speaks of when he says, "Das Äusere ist ein in einen Geheimniszustand aufgehobenes Innere." (The outer world is the inner world, raised to a condition of secrecy.)

It's difficult to find our way into this condition of secrecy. Of course we dream of being able to say that it happens as easily and lightly as a plant sprouts leaves and flowers. So that the poem in the seed's internal sky is lifted into its whole outer unfolding as exactly that plant, exactly that poem.

In this condition of secrecy, the poet stands at the center of a universe that has no center. In order to raise the inner world to the outer we have to start in the outer, start in all that's visible, everything that throughout our whole lives, in corresponding forms of visibility, has been preserved yet forgotten in our inner world. It's unclear which has to awaken which, the inner or the outer, but it's certain that— because we know how things have been connected with each other ever since we were children—our first and best help will come from random chance: maybe in the form of a spring rain or an autumn storm, summer's bright nights or winter's rime frost, any phenomenon at all that can set our inner world in motion to such a degree that threads, pathways of thoughts, are created, branching out and trying to find ways to fuse words and phenomena.

Before we sit down with our paper in order to (maybe, maybe not) write a poem, as well as during the many hours we sit there, that's the way it is: as if we've become lost. The world, which a moment ago, when we were drinking our morning coffee, was perfectly manageable and normal, has once more suddenly become far too big, and even if our consciousness wanders in all directions, bringing its small bits of language along, it can't locate exactly the stone, the plant, the situation, perhaps the incomprehensibility, from which it can find its way back to the world with the aid of a word.

Sometimes it helps to avert our gaze and simply listen to the sounds and rhythms of words, feel our way and listen to that music for so long that we eventually know the music itself has a meaning needing only to be lured out; so the words aren't left on their own in their own melodiousness, but through this steadfast listening, this freighting of flow, speed, and color, can at last be brought forth through our astonished eyes to meet the spring rain or the rime frost or whatever it is, and can begin to gather new words and seen or unseen things.

That's how it is in the beginning: great anxiety and confusion, but also patience with our fear of leaping in, because we know that others have made the leap before us. Deep inside we know that the beginning is a bridge already built, even though it's not until we step out into empty space that we can feel the bridge beneath our feet.

The fear of stepping out into empty space is understandable. It's true that the history of poetry includes maps of all kinds of landscapes, with all possible bridges sketched in, but at the moment when we have to take the first step, we realize that this specific landscape has moved, or the bridge has moved; either they've both moved at once or they've each moved separately; and the map, which otherwise seemed indispensable as an overview of all of world literature, is now functioning only as a possibility, maybe just a suggestion, of how some landscape or other might conceivably look on the day we get there. So we really are lost, in a very odd way. We need to find our way through the landscape in order to draw the map, and at the same time we need to draw the map in order to find our way through the landscape.

It's here, as we're realizing that the bridge has to be built before we make a move, that we have to choose our words with care. And *care* doesn't necessarily mean "carefulness." It can also mean courage and determination, clear-sightedness and generosity. We can inch forward or leap for all we're worth, and either way we'll find that there is solid ground beneath our feet. We can creep and crawl, dance and sway, or give ourselves over to walking completely normally. Under any circumstances, the only thing that means anything, if we choose our words with that kind of care, is that phenomena meet the words, so the bridge can be walked on and the empty space filled with a landscape.

Choosing with care also means more than choosing among all random words. We have to choose exactly the random word that can be made necessary. To make a word necessary means to interweave or fuse it with its phenomenon. Not that the randomness is done away with, because even after we choose it, the word is still as random as ever. But in its randomness the word, along with the phenomenon, will enter into that condition of secrecy where inner and outer worlds exist together, as if they had never been separated.

When the first stations have been set up in this condition of secrecy, the poem begins to take shape, the landscape broadens out, and images begin, on their own, to keep words and phenomena together. Where before there was nothing, now there is something; and along with it something else that continues the process, because all the widespread outposts in the landscape start to report in, all the little enclaves of coinciding language and meaning that now are functioning as realities, everything that has entered into the condition of secrecy, reports back now and shows unequivocally not only how we should write but first and foremost why and what we *can* write, what was always meant to be written about, even if along the way we thought, or maybe frankly hoped, that it was something completely different.

Over time, many poets have tried to describe this inconceivable situation, and their statements almost always center on something about having the words suddenly take over, or finding that the poem writes itself, things along those lines.

At any rate we're no longer staring at the words "cloud layer," for example, or at the cloud layer itself in the sky outside, and wondering if it should or shouldn't be part of the poem. That was already determined long before.

In the same way, regardless of the decision about using the words "cloud layer," it's already been determined whether or not that's really what we're writing about. Because at the very moment that the words take over, it's the poem's images, comparisons, and relationships that decide whether a word should be included or not, in order for what's written about to be precisely that word.

And at the happy moment when all decisions become part and parcel of the poem's writing of itself, it may even be decided that what's being written about is something we had never remotely considered writing about, something we'd completely forgotten, something we'd never spoken of, something that has kept itself hidden until now, finally luring our consciousness out with some important thing like war, peace, happiness, death, and so on, all signs that those big words have their own inaccessible condition of secrecy: for example, the war that for years, long before our piece of writing started, we had grown used to thinking and feeling was permanently impossible to write about—impossible in a poem, at any rate.

When I chose to write about this condition of secrecy in terms of writing poetry, it was definitely not because there's anything special about poetry.

Poetry is just one of human beings' many ways of recognizing things, and the same schism runs through each of the other ways, be it philosophy, mathematics, or the natural sciences.

There is a schism between those who believe that we human beings, with our language, are set apart from the world, and those who experience human beings' use of language as part of the world, so it becomes evident that whenever we express ourselves through language, the world too is expressing itself.

We probably all hear on a daily basis that the condition of the rainforests—their life, and their breathing—are expressions of the condition of the planet. But why shouldn't another expression of the condition of the planet be the way that we human beings live and breathe and express ourselves—and that, for example, expresses the condition of the rainforests?

We need to realize that we can't set ourselves apart from the world. We can act as if we could. But the fact that we can act as if we could is yet another aspect of that which we can't set ourselves apart from. We can't recognize anything without using recognition itself.

Wars—including those of ideology—can be waged only because people believe that it's possible to set themselves apart and to cordon off a specific reality.

Occasionally, I wish there were a weather report for human beings' motions, for the motion of the mind that causes us to topple walls, the hunger that causes us to wander like denuded trees through desert sands, the white-collar swarm that attracts us like insects to the stock market—I don't understand why the heights of recognition haven't brought me the weather report that would explain all these human high pressure areas, or low pressure areas, or human cyclones that are part of the current condition of the planet.

Especially since I've learned from meteorologists and other scientists I've met that they know about the condition of secrecy. They may not say that words suddenly take over, but they say that the problem suddenly solves itself; they don't say that a poem writes itself, no, but they do say that things *say* themselves.

They plug away for years, trying to get consciousness and vision to hang together, and slog endlessly around assorted university campuses, until the world suddenly inscribes itself in them and the difference between human being and world vanishes, so the world can write itself by means of human consciousness.

This is possible only because we're bound to the forms of nature, in that we ourselves are one of its manifold forms.

This is why recognizing the connections and interrelatedness among all the things in the world isn't restricted only to poets, scientists, or others who cultivate the relationship between consciousness and the world.

That recognition is already built into the world. Into all the comparisons that the world itself consists of. For instance, it's inconceivable that we humans could go without saying, at one time or another, that apples are round just as the sun is round, or without making innumerable similar comparisons.

The whole web of relationships among all the phenomena that make up our world leads us to an increasingly refined understanding that our forms of culture—all the forms of expression that humans have created, including the many kinds of poetry—can certainly be considered things in themselves, but above all else they are forms of nature.

This is why I'm appealing to our sense of being borne up by an inconceivably huge, already existing foundation of comparisons. Specifically to our awareness that we as poets must learn to love prepositions—words that express relationships among phenomena—because prepositions, almost unreasonably invisible though they are, keep our consciousness in the same kind of motion as the world.

So self-realization—for example as a poet—just to feel that something exists in the world, becomes entirely unnecessary, as opposed to de-realizing ourselves, because everything already exists in the world. There is also a kind of comfort in that. If we're separate from the world, it's because we have separated ourselves. We believe as much. But we mustn't believe as much. We must know. That we already are in the condition of secrecy we seek.

(1992)

In the Beginning Was the Flesh

Everything has always already begun. The day I realized that I could stand up and walk, I had already been moving around in the world for quite a while. The day I realized what it actually was that I was eating, I had already been consuming the broadest assortment of things for quite a while. The day I realized that human beings are constantly realizing things, my brain had already been busy with the oddest ideas for quite a while. And it still is, I assume. I hope. I wouldn't be surprised if right now, while I'm writing this, it were covertly manipulating the fragments that it's stumbled across along our way, trying to arrange them a bit better. So that some day I might be able to wander among them fairly effortlessly. So that some day I might sit down and write something that I don't know I already know.

I'd like to tell a little about the fragments that I do know I stumbled across while I was writing the volume of poetry titled *It*. And maybe also about how their arrangement got a bit better.

FRAGMENT #1. 1965. An essay by Lars Gustafsson, "The Problem of the Long Poem," in the journal *BLM*. Its effect on me was to challenge and invite. Among other things, he wrote:

1: "The problem of the long poem lies in the struggle with the poem's length. It arises from the need to unify the long lines, the details, the complexity, and the experience of simultaneity, keeping them all intact."

2: "Can we imagine principles of form whose choice of certain fundamental elements determines those same elements' recurrence elsewhere in the poem—but what is repeated or varied is neither words nor lines, more like compositional patterns or attitudes?"

3: "If we have enough in common, in the sum of our experiences as they appear in our concepts, in the gestalt of our sciences, in our views of society and tradition, if we have enough common points of departure, then these can provide the foundation for a functional allegorical poem, which in its multiple meanings can encompass both what is factual and what is self-reflective."

I thought that nothing less would do. Nothing less than that attempt.

FRAGMENT #2. Around the same time. Or maybe a little later. An exhibit at Charlottenborg Gallery in Copenhagen, of a series of images by the Swedish graphic artist Per-Gunnar Thelander.

His point of departure was Botticelli's *The Birth of Venus*—that charming, stately, otherworldly lady, washed clean and born of sea-foam, who glides ashore as calmly as if nothing at all out of the ordinary were happening, standing on a symmetrical white seashell in the midst of the unlikeliest blue.

Thelander had copied Botticelli's Venus exactly. The copy was not particularly big, and it was set at a slight angle, as if it were just some art postcard that happened to turn up on his drawing board.

But there the process began in earnest. Again. As the first, the "real Venus," rose from her sea-foam and landed on Botticelli's canvas, in the same way Botticelli's "real Venus" landed back in her true element. Like the image she had become, she was copied and developed, cropped and highlighted in every possible way. She went from chemical bath to chemical bath and was twisted and turned, manipulated, laid out to dry on newspapers in draft after draft, until the woman being born was also the woman giving birth, until the mouth giving birth was also the mouth that speaks, and until the hand shifting the images became the hand that lifts the wisps of foam up to its owner's mouth, which blows this Venus upward like a bubble. Venus #117, the "real" one lifting herself up by the hair.

When I saw those images, I wanted Thelander to do the cover of my next book of poetry. And on a little piece of paper, I wrote, "Photocells ... Biological principles used as words. A growing organism of water, stone, and words."

FRAGMENT #3. My acquaintance with Noam Chomsky's basic principles of generative grammar and transformational grammar, his ideas of an innate faculty for language and of universal rules for structuring sentences, rules that determine linguistic structure but that simultaneously allow the generation of infinite sentences. Chomsky's vision of language gave me a feeling of fantastic happiness. A proof beyond proof that language is a direct extension of nature. That I had the same "right" to produce language that a tree has to produce leaves. If I could just start in total silence, slip into the first sentences, hide there as in water, flowing, go on until the first little ripples appeared, almost words, almost sentences, more and more.

Toward the end of *It*, there's a poem that reflects this security:

> *I see the weightless clouds*
> *I see the weightless sun*
> *I see how easily they trace*
> *An endless course*
>
> *As if they trust in me*
> *Here on the earth*
> *As if they know that I*
> *Am their words*

But back when I was collecting those fragments, I was nowhere near the end of *It*. I wasn't even at the beginning. I wasn't even thinking yet of starting. It was May of 1967, and I was working on my novel *Azorno*. It happened suddenly: on the day I finished, got the manuscript in order, and slipped it into an envelope, I heard myself say, "It. That's it." And during the course of the evening I kept going with that—which became the beginning of *It*.

It didn't take me long to realize that it was a kind of creation story. I could tell, by the way those little sentences moved and by the way they constantly referred to each other and to their own movement, and only to that movement, that they would put up terrific resistance if I suddenly, arbitrarily forced a person into them, for example, or a city, or any other random thing. I had to start at the very beginning, and gradually let things fill in more and more, so that it all could unfold naturally.

Then I started thinking a little about this sentence: "In the beginning was the Word ... and the Word was made flesh." I thought, what if we could think the unthinkable: that flesh could speak, that one cell could signal to another, so that the whole inarticulate world suddenly partook in the following impossible (to human awareness) experience: In the beginning was the flesh, and the flesh was made words ...

And in my attempt to keep a firm grip on the concurrent duality of those two sentences, those paradoxical conditions, I began to produce something that I myself was a product of.

In the beginning I actually acted as if I weren't there, as if it ("I") were just a bit of flesh talking, a bit of protoplasm, acted as if *I* were just following along, while a language, a world, took shape. That's why I called the first part PROLOGOS: the part, even if it's only fictive, that comes before the word, before consciousness. Background, starting point, vantage point. Prologue, in the theater.

After that it made sense to call the "piece" itself LOGOS. The word as creative principle. The place where things are consciously staged, put into action, into relationship.

And then I would have been stymied if I hadn't gotten hold of *Præpositioners teori* (A Theory of Prepositions) by Viggo Brøndal. His attempt to analyze and categorize the words that languages use to show relationship can be read as applying to the network of relationships that writing builds up as it goes along. From his book I chose eight terms that could stay in a state of flux and at the same time give order to the indistinctness that a state of flux necessarily must produce: *symmetry, transitivity, continuity, connectivity, variability, extension, integrity,* and *universality.*

I noticed that, concerning *universality,* Brøndal had written, "The most wide-ranging synthesis would ultimately encompass all zones and degrees of relationship: abstract, concrete, and complex; primary and secondary; central and peripheral. That kind of total relationship must, in keeping with its nature, exist at the boundaries of thought; as an expression of the quality of experience, it must be of an almost mystical character."

And when the piece is over, there's the EPILOGOS. After the word. Where I could act as if the word weren't the creative principle, as if the word were only communication. That's how it was. Or: that's how it seemed to me that it was (is).

As life is a writing within death.

(1970)

It's All Words

The word creates what it names." But what does it mean when we say that a word, by naming something, creates that something? Can I, just by mentioning the word *rose*, bring a rose into being somewhere? No, of course I can't say "rose" and poof, hocus-pocus, a rose appears in the visible world. That kind of thing happens only in the world of fairy tales, where things regularly happen as soon as the right word is said: "Hocus pocus," and the rose hedge bursts into bloom; "Open, sesame," and the mountain opens; "Table, set yourself," and all sorts of the tastiest dishes are served forth; "And God said, Let there be light: and there was light."

But, as I said, that kind of thing happens only in the world of fairy tales—in the world of fantasy, the whole world of our thoughts and imaginings. And in this inner world, the word does create what it names.

It's in this world of imaginings that I can say "rose," and if I close my eyes, a rose will appear before my inner eye, maybe not entirely as visible as it would be in a garden, but visible, and if I open my eyes again and say "rose," as I'm doing while I prepare this talk, one rose after another will appear, a whole world of roses, in my memory: the first rose that a boyfriend ever gave me, the bouquet of roses when my son was born, rose gardens here and there in the world, the great rose window in Sainte-Chapelle in Paris, and the rose catalog I used when I was writing my novel *Azorno*, all those rose names: "Rosa hugonis, Rosa pimpinellifolia, Blaze Superior, Virgo and Rosa rugosa, Rosa rubiginosa, Rosa 'Nevada.' These continuous destructions"—and soon all those words would be so busy creating what they name that I would be tempted to toss aside the draft of my talk and write a long string of rose poems instead.

As I resist the temptation to set this talk aside, I realize that the way it now begins is not at all the way I intended to begin, because I originally wanted to start with "In the beginning was the Word, and the Word was with God, and the Word was God"—but now it's too late. And maybe that's a very good thing.

Because I notice that the way I've actually begun is already busy putting its mark on the coming course of the talk—a mark that, even as I was inserting the verse from the Gospel of John, is changing that verse, and giving me permission to leave John the Evangelist to the theologians, and to focus on John the poet.

To focus specifically on his bold phrase "the Word was God" as a foundation for the concept that "the word creates what it names," and to interpret his statements first and foremost as an introduction to a story about what creation is, and then afterward to a story about how the world was created.

Seen in that way it becomes a matter of humans' faith in the word as such, in its innate magic, its self-generating ability to create an imaginary world. John the poet knew all this when he wrote his introductory verse, and he especially knew that it's all words. But where do the words come from?

As it is now, when the world has existed for so long, words come from everywhere, and they're never there for the first time. Not only that. Although there may not be an infinite number of them, nor an infinite number of combinations, nevertheless there is an inexhaustible landscape of words, there are more than any one individual could manage to travel through. This is where it ends and where it begins, if a person is going to write poems: in the imagined concept of this mysterious landscape. For poems are created exclusively from words.

Right away, why and how they're created becomes a far more complex matter. But just as the artist has her paints, the composer his musical notes, and the mathematician her numbers and formulae, which are, in principle, things that every human being has, in the same way the poet has his words, which are things that every human being has not only in principle, but also in practice.

So then why doesn't everyone write poems? Since we all do possess enough words—in fact an abundance, a veritable excess of words.

It's understandable that not everyone paints; paints are expensive, and it's a lot of trouble to live with all the equipment in a studio apartment. And in the same way it's understandable that not everyone composes music, because musical instruments are expensive, too, and none of us learn musical notation in daycare. And later, mathematics becomes too hard—among other reasons, because schools make it too hard and too exotic. But words—we can all understand them, and we have them with us everywhere, so to create poems all we really need is paper and something to write with—actually not even that, because I can imagine that if I were in some prison or somewhere else without access to paper, I'd try to write poems in my mind, and every day I'd work on memorizing them, possibly by muttering them out loud to the nearest cockroach.

And that may be what the question boils down to. Is it at all possible to learn to write poems in a way that will make it seem important to read them out loud to a cockroach? Is it even possible to prepare for that extreme situation? A situation that can also be privileged, though psychologically very exposed and vulnerable. As Rilke writes:

> *Exposed upon the mountains of the heart. Look, how small*
> *   there!*
> *look: the last village of words, and higher,*

but again how small, still one last
homestead of feeling. Can you make it out?

We can ask, then, if it's possible to learn to be "exposed upon the mountains of the heart." Isn't that just something we are, something we're born into, a destiny that we take on because we can't do anything else, or because there isn't anything else we can do?

Can we learn to create a destiny, or is a destiny something we learn how to have because it's what we've been granted?

This question may not require an examination of the word *destiny*, nor of everything either granted or self-created in our lives, but rather an examination of the meaning of *learn*.

Learn, in German *lernen*, comes from the Proto-Germanic root *leisjan*, "make known by searching." That root comes from Proto-Germanic *lais*, "I know, have traveled through, have experienced," and is also related to the root of the German word *leisten* (accomplish), which originally meant "to follow a trail/track," and which comes very close to our theme here: that language, merely by existing, offers poets (among others) myriad tracks, tracks that become reality by being followed.

This is hard to explain, especially in words: how words, as one follows these imaginary tracks, find their place in a poem being written. And of course it's no easier to describe what these word-places in a poem mean.

But I think I found some help with this as I was reading Bruce Chatwin's book *The Songlines*. In Danish, the book is called *Drømmespor*, "Dreamtracks," a title that fits the content perfectly.

Bruce Chatwin tells of "the labyrinth of invisible pathways which meander all over Australia and are known to Europeans as 'Dreaming-tracks' or 'Songlines'; to the Aboriginals as the 'Footprints of the Ancestors' or the 'Way of the Law.'"

Here the Aboriginals tell creation stories about "the legendary totemic beings who had wandered over the country in the Dreamtime, singing out the name of everything that crossed their path—birds, animals, plants, rocks, water holes—and so singing the world into existence."

The Australian Aboriginals believe that they must recreate the world again and again by singing it, or else it will stop existing. "An unsung land is a dead land: since, if the songs are forgotten, the land itself will die"—and along with it, of course, the people. This is why, year after year, they must travel these same tracks and sing into being now a stone, now a tree, now a water hole, a desert plant, not because these phenomena exist, but literally in order for them to arise, to continually be brought into existence, so to speak, and accumulate memorability. For me, that's a very tangible example of the word creating what it names.

And that's why it's not especially hard for me to compare this advanced Australian technique with a modern, or perhaps timeless, way to write poems.

We can say that luckily or unluckily I don't have to wander through the Australian outback and with my words sing forth or conjure up all the things in the world so that they emerge into the light of day or directly "enter into existence," as Kierkegaard would say. Yet as a poet I do face a sort of Australian outback—the blank page—and within the blank page, the invisible dream tracks, the writing of all those who came before, and in my hands a writing implement that hesitates for a very long time, because if stone-age people's songlines are to be included in what is written, then I must listen not only to the arbitrary present moment, but also to all times past, and to so many people besides myself, as if the paper had become a huge space with all possible kinds of tracks.

That is the poet's classic situation. The hours-long, maybe days-long confrontation with the blank page, and with the awareness that "In the beginning was the word," but which word? The word that will instantly start transforming nothingness into everything.

For in the beginning there is nothing but the blank page. Not a word.

But as soon as there's even a handful of words, though there's still almost nothing there, the blank page is totally transformed. What at first was an ordinary sheet of paper—and could easily have been made into a paper airplane—now becomes a sheet of paper that's in the process of being filled with words. This is not only because I can't even write "there's nothing on this page" without something being on the page; it's also because by doing that, I'm also writing that I expect it to change soon, I expect that words will fill the page, which they eventually do, to such an extent that the page goes, all on its own, from being a piece of paper with nothing on it to being an image of the nothingness that once was nowhere, but that is now between the lines and in the spaces between the words.

In that way, we can regard the page as an image of the great nothingness where everything exists, uncreated. Not because everything isn't there; it's just that the hidden and forgotten and unbounded possibility that it is can't be brought forth without the help of words.

Since words, in that way, manage to establish their own written world on the page, the whiteness between the words not only will remain white, but also—because the words are chosen from among countless possibilities—it will appear more and more to be the mandatory backdrop, or abyss, of nothingness that the arbitrariness of the words indicates.

I've experienced that myself, in a deeply upsetting way; I've sat facing that nothingness and had no idea which way to turn. Without as much as a single track to follow. A condition where all the words in the world and all the phenomena in the world were totally isolated from themselves and from each other, and where no matter which word's door I knocked at, no meaning came forth.

Here it would be natural to put a question mark after the claim that poems are brought forth exclusively from words and from nothingness, in the form of the blank page.

We want the solace of imagining that a poem might describe an experience the poet has had, an episode from daily life or maybe from travel, an unparalleled sunset, or any other thing at all; or that a poem could build on thoughts the poet has had, for example ideas about how a social system should be structured, or musings about connections among all living creatures on earth.

But poems aren't made out of experiences, or out of thoughts, ideas, or musings about anything. Poems are made out of words.

It's through our listening to the words, to their rhythms and timbres, the entirety of their music, that the meanings in them can be set free.

It's through our fascination with words, through our marveling at them, at these remarkable human sounds and their broadly encompassing network of interrelationships, that poems can happen at all.

Along these lines, Novalis, in his "Monologue" from 1798, writes beautifully about his insight into the poet's relationship to language: "Matters concerning speech and writing are genuinely strange: proper conversation is a mere play of words. We can only marvel at the laughable error people make—believing that they speak about things. No one knows precisely what is peculiar to language, that it concerns itself merely with itself. For that reason, it is a wonderful and fertile mystery—when someone speaks merely in order to speak, one expresses precisely then the most splendid and most original truths. Yet if one wishes to speak of something determinate, then temperamental language has him say the most laughable and perverse things."

Later he continues, "If only one could make people grasp that the case of language is similar to that of mathematical formulae—they constitute a world for themselves, they play with themselves alone, express nothing other than their wonderful nature, and precisely for that reason they are so expressive—precisely for that reason they mirror in themselves the curious play of relations in things."

The whole monologue ends with Novalis's assertion about writers, stated as the last part of a question: "... inasmuch as a writer is only an enthusiast of language?" (The German *Begeisterung* means enthusiasm, inspiration.)

At this point I'd like to turn back to the impossible situation that I experienced, which I mentioned earlier. It happened around 1980, when I was writing, or rather was not yet understanding how I was going to write, the collection of poems called *alphabet*. I really was sitting in front of a blank sheet of paper, as an almost insanely enthusiastic "enthusiast of language," whose enthusiasm was leading absolutely nowhere.

Because, of course, poems are written only with words. But definitely, only if the words can also come to mean something. And there are situations, crises in the individual and in the world, when no word, no matter how beautiful it sounds, can come to have any meaning at all.

Why write, when the blank page behind the words just gets blanker and blanker? Why write, when the Cold War was at its very coldest and human beings were thinking up more and more irrevocable ways to wipe themselves out?

Why write, if no one craved poems anymore—if all they craved was blank, white, all-destroying nothingness?

Those may sound like rhetorical questions now, but at the time it was like suffering from a high fever.

The work had started as a process of collecting words. A drive that I myself didn't understand, to write, on sheets and sheets of paper, individual words, preferably nouns, linked to concrete phenomena in the world, everything edible, visible, smellable, available to the senses: apricots, doves, melons, and so on. There they sat, those words, on big pieces of white paper, words starting with *a*, with *b*, with *c*, and so on, and if I'd kept at it much longer it would have looked like an odd, unorganized dictionary, a wilderness of unrelated phenomena.

Nevertheless, it eventually became clear to me that it was a matter of weaving a kind of spell. A prayer that apricots, doves, melons, and so on could continue to exist in the world. And at the same time, a prayer that atom bombs, hydrogen bombs, dioxin, and so on could disappear.

But a dictionary, much less a large collection of words on paper, just doesn't add up to spell-weaving. Only to potential readers possessed of the ultimate goodwill and imagination could I have presented an arbitrary group of words, all starting with *a*, for instance, on an 8½" by 11" sheet of paper, as if it were a poem.

It was then that mathematics came to my rescue.

For, since phenomena themselves never occur in a complete context just because they're given names, it was my good fortune that during my search for words (in a dictionary, under *f*) I happened to stumble upon numbers—specifically, the Fibonacci numbers—which I experienced almost as a mystical vision, an image of the origin and development of the universe, answering to the Big Bang theory, the leading theory at the time. According to the Big Bang theory, here's what happened when the universe was born: everything, at first compressed into next to nothing, exploded. It began spreading to all sides, and it will continue spreading until the distances become so great that it will all seem to disappear and become nothing again, or next to nothing.

An image, then. Or a vision of the world as a context that's mute in terms of words, but that has, in terms of numbers, very telling links among various phenomena, a context and a beauty evidenced, for example, by the fact that Fibonacci numbers are literally present in the growth principles of many kinds of plants, each number in the Fibonacci series coming from the sum of the two previous numbers, so that the numbers grow extremely fast, an exponential curve traveling at top speed toward infinity, but at the same time coming closer and closer to what we humans call the Golden Mean.

So then it felt like a great adventure to try to combine this wordless universal poem of numbers with the man-made alphabet, or more accurately, to imply the combination by means of an unfinished series of poems.

And why make the writing of poetry so complicated? One possible answer: it may be precisely what's very complicated that's the most simple. A rose, when we think about it, is very complicated, but still very simple. "A rose is a rose is a rose," as Gertrude Stein says, her insistent repetition highlighting the mystery in the existence of the rose and of language itself.

Normally we think of a rose as made by nature, a part of nature's self-realization, while we think of language as man-made, something that we alone hold the patent on.

But just as we ourselves are a part of the remarkable biology project that makes the earth unique, at least in our part of the universe, so too is language a part of that biology project.

Applying this line of thought doesn't mean that we lose free will and can shift the blame for every problem onto biology. We're still the ones who can write anything and everything, and invent anything and everything, both for good and for ill; but only at a certain level. At a different level, both free will and language lose all meaning. Even the existence of the sun, the fact that it's burning and will finally burn itself up, and similarly even the existence of death, makes our everyday death here on the earth an illustration that we can indeed decide all sorts of things, but only because we decide nothing. If we really could decide everything, we wouldn't be here at all, simply because we'd have no reason to want to survive.

For a long time now, our attempts to survive have managed to make it look like language belongs only to us. As if the word were entirely our own invention, designed to conjure up and master the world around us. Now we've finally come so far in that mastery that we're discovering how our mastery is mastering us. And here I'm not talking about self-mastery, because we still haven't figured out how to do that, at any rate not when we're together.

Maybe that's why I'm pursuing this idea. Because I don't feel that it diminishes human beings in any way to say we need only listen to the music of the word in order to hear that it too is created by something beyond us. Without the word necessarily being called divine.

But the word must necessarily be called dual. Dual, meaning being both inside and outside. Inside the consciousness that calls some things divine, but simultaneously outside, in the divinity that calls consciousness forth. And within the poem a constant conversation between those two levels must be carried on.

Maybe the function of the word can be described in an image: a membrane between inside and outside, a membrane that regulates the osmotic exchange between consciousness and the surrounding world.

And not until enough words have found their places in the poem, and thus enough has been left out, which is the most important thing in life, and brought forth, and general knowledge is connected to in-born knowledge, when these things and many more have happened as words are pulled from thin air or from library shelves, recycling upon recycling, not until then will balance finally be reached, the osmotic pressure equalized, and the membrane cease to function. The word wholly itself.

That doesn't mean that we can no longer enter into conversation with the poem. Just the opposite. It means that at least temporarily, a balance has been achieved between inside and outside, that the membrane has been made impermeable—to write poems means to create impermeability—in the sense that there's no longer any striving to reach and master another level; everything in the poem seems held in suspension, in constant motion yet quite still, as in the eye of a storm, in what Novalis calls "das seltsame Verhältnisspiel der Dinge" (the strange interrelatedness of things).

And this is definitely a condition very much worth striving for, one that human beings will go to great lengths to achieve. Because maybe for us this condition, which ultimately renders the world understandable, doesn't actually exist unless words give it a name and thereby create it, again and again, before our wondering eyes.

(1992)

The Naive Reader

When I write poems, I sometimes pretend it's not me but language itself that's writing.

I pretend it's possible to step back a bit from my human persona and to observe language from the outside, as if I myself had never used it.

I pretend language and the world have their own connection. Pretend the individual words, without me, are directly related to the phenomena they refer to. So that it becomes possible for the world to find its own meaning. A meaning that's already there.

This is just something I pretend. But I also feel that it's something I need to do. I need to find meaning in the world, not because I've dedicated myself to doing it, maybe not even because I want to do it, but because I, like any of the world's other native inhabitants, can't help creating meaning, the meaning that is already there and that unceasingly manages its own transformation, in the process that we call survival.

I can put it another way. My expressing myself here is no different in principle from a tree growing leaves. Self-producing, self-regulating biological systems are basically the same, whether they're called trees or humans.

As a human, naturally I have to admit that as I sit here by my window, I can see a tree, whereas the tree presumably can't see me. But what does "see" mean? That's human language. Of course it's correct to say that the tree hasn't seen anything, yet in its own way the tree has seen me, nevertheless. It has registered human presence, even if as nothing more than air pollution.

Then we could say this basically just shows that humans are more fully developed than trees and have power over things; that we're the ones who can decide whether trees will die, and not vice versa. But who knows how the transformation might best be managed? Maybe what looks like forest die-off is, more than anything else, a sign that we ourselves are in danger, that we ourselves could perish—after the forests do, of course.

But whether it happens before or after is, for that matter, less relevant to the trees' welfare than to our own. After all, we haven't demonstrated any ability to rise again from the earth after we die, whereas seeds that have lain hidden in the Egyptian pyramids have been shown to be viable today. So we can assume that trees will just hide in the earth and come up again in due time, sometime when air pollution and humans are gone. The trees will survive, though in that event, more likely in the company of cockroaches than of us.

Of course that's no way to see it. And yet. Maybe it shows that in actuality, the world can both read and be read. That impressions can be harvested just as grapes can. That signs can be gathered just as nourishment can. That we as humans can read a multitude of signs, from the motions of the stars and the clouds, through the migrations of birds and shoals of fish, to the language of ants and of the swirling of water at home in the kitchen sink. Everything from astronomy and invisible chemistry to biology and its climates. But ants too read. Trees too read and know within seconds when they should let their leaves droop, if their blossoming is endangered.

Still, we are, of course, unique. But only because the earth is unique. It's the earth that has, in its biosphere, drafted the project called humanity, which is unique not so much because there are no others like us in our vicinity in space, and not so much because we can interpret sign systems and try to convert them to our own language, nor because we can read the natural and historical progression of readability itself—no, essentially we're unique only because we use the word *god*.

Because we have to imagine that we ourselves, after all our reading of ourselves and of everything else, ultimately will reach the boundary of readability. And it may be this boundary, perceived in advance, that makes us unique. It's at this boundary, which actually lies deep within our own thoughts, that we in passing carry on the conversation between readability and unreadability that we provisionally call *god*.

And we have been carrying on that conversation for a long time. Since before we ever had a written language. Maybe almost before we had a spoken language. In any case before we composed the first poem, oral or written, because we already were aligned with the poem that is the universe's own.

Along the way we've made various attempts to capture that poem, and we've called it everything from divine revelation to science. From the first holy scriptures that came into the world, such as the Bible, on through Novalis to Mallarmé, and in science on to the latest theories of the workings of the universe, a concept of the book of the world has existed, the book that expresses everything and thus halts the conversation between readability and unreadability within the word *god*. So to speak.

A concept that has always drawn sustenance from its own impossibility. It's true that the Bible is called divine revelation, but it is a revelation funneling into the provision that "now we see through a glass, darkly, but then we shall see face to face"—"then" meaning at some future time when the world being revealed no longer exists.

And when Novalis searches for the all-encompassing fusion of words and phenomena—"Das Äussere ist ein in einen Geheimniszustand erhobenes Innere" ("The outer world is an inner world raised to a condition of secrecy")—and works his way toward the formula for that archetypal book, the task grows like wild weeds, because of course the more he gathers of it all, or reads his way into it all, the more it seems to spread, just as, later, Mallarmé too begins to direct his attention more toward the emptiness between words than toward the words themselves.

And when science tries to write the book of the world, its attempts on the whole consist of constantly revised theories about the origin of the universe, its inner design and workings, theories that arise right at that same boundary, where the conversation between readability and unreadability can be carried on perfectly well, using terms such as chaos theory, fractals, and superstrings—but only because the word *god* sounds too overbearing.

But just as the letters within a book will never be able to read the book, we will never be able to read the world. Of course, the letters wouldn't try. We, by contrast, are bound to keep reading. And for us it will always be like Borges's famous story about the map of the world that's constantly being enlarged and made more detailed, until ultimately it's as big as the whole world and conceals what it was originally intended to reveal.

In the human dimension the map must remain an abbreviation. And in the same way, language must remain an abbreviation for the world's readability per se. A poetic abbreviation for all the sign systems in the universe, whose relationship and movements we can't avoid reading. What Novalis calls "das seltsame Verhältnisspiel der Dinge" ("the strange interplay of things") and all the relationships in the world. This interplay of relationships is expressed in all sorts of self-producing systems and the ways they're interwoven. In the human world, first and foremost, in language and mathematics as they're interwoven within us. Among other things, in the form of poems.

If we provisionally pretend that the universe can read and write itself, we find ourselves in the middle of the poem called the Big Bang Theory. At the dawn of the universe, here's what happened: everything, which at first was compressed into next to nothing (somewhere between 0 and 1), exploded and spread to all sides, a motion that will continue until everything is spread so very thin that it will seem to disappear and become nothing again, or next to nothing. An image. Or a poem situated far out in unreadability, at the same time that we with our human language suggest that it could be able to read itself.

But whether poems are written in one way or the other—whether I pretend it's me or language itself doing the writing, whether I straightforwardly read the world or say that I, reading the world, am part of the world, and thus it is reading itself—regardless, I am and will remain the naive reader, a native inhabitant, an insider who can never see her world from the outside. And my poem will relate to the universe in the same way the eye relates to its own retina. But still, it sees. And it keeps reading.

(1991)

The Regulating Effect of Chance

One day on the Copenhagen metro I heard the following exchange between two older women:

"All those random possibilities—there shouldn't be any need for that."

"No, there shouldn't. They should put a stop to it. There's way too much being left to chance."

I didn't hear what they were talking about. It could have been anything. And the exchange could have taken place between any two people. For despite its everyday tone, it encompasses basic truths about humans' relationship to chance and necessity. This becomes more evident when we formulate the two abstract questions concealed beneath the women's unsettling and testy remarks. First, is chance necessary? And second, is chance the prevailing force?

To take the second question first: is chance the prevailing force? The answer, as far as it's possible to know, has to be yes. The universe, which includes the earth and all life here on earth, exists under chance conditions, regardless of how necessary, orderly, and subject to natural laws everything around us seems, from the life cycles of plants to the orbit of the earth around the sun, aside from certain deviations such as volcanoes, human behavior, etc.

What chance itself actually is, of course, we have no idea. We know only that there's something we call chance. That there's something we perceive as chance. So there might well also be things about chance that we don't perceive. It may even be full of order, just an order that broadcasts on frequencies other than those our human senses can pick up.

We're living, then, under these remarkable, chance conditions, which Jacques Monod describes strikingly in his *Chance & Necessity*:

> Among all the occurrences possible in the universe, the *a priori* possibility of any particular one of them verges upon zero. Yet the universe exists; particular events must take place in it, the probability of which (before the event) was infinitesimal. At the present time we have no legitimate grounds for either asserting or denying that life got off to but a single start on earth, and that, as a consequence, before it appeared its chances of occurring were next to nil.
>
> Not only for scientific reasons do biologists recoil at this idea. It runs counter to our very human tendency to believe that behind everything real in the world stands a necessity rooted in the very beginning of things. Against this notion, this powerful feeling of destiny, we must be constantly on guard.

The two women on the metro were not. They were not on guard against any feeling of destiny. They were just expressing the human tendency to believe in our own feeling that we are necessities, the feeling that leads us to try to combat, control, or subsume chance, perhaps in the hope of ultimately overpowering it and seeing it disappear.

In this way, we admit that chance is indeed the prevailing force, but at the same time we experience an overwhelming need to eradicate it. In our daily lives we simply act as if we actually were necessities, and as if we dictated the conditions of chance, rather than vice versa.

We might want to ask ourselves whether eradicating chance really is so crucial to our feeling of being necessary, even to our survival. Can't we imagine feeling just as necessary if we face chance squarely? Maybe feeling even more necessary, if we dare to look directly at the ways that chance exerts its control?

This is where I think the first of the two original questions comes in. The woman on the metro said "there shouldn't be any need for" chance. The underlying message: it *ought* not to be necessary, but it apparently *is*. Formulated as a question—is chance necessary?—is it in reality a needed working partner, a kind of neutral helper that, if we gain insight into its essence, could change our thinking, and therefore our lives, for the better? Maybe we could conceive of it as a kind of inexhaustible layer of white noise from which, in principle, music can always be drawn, just not always exactly when the individual wants it or feels that it's necessary—more likely when the individual dares to let go, for the briefest instant, of his own feeling of being necessary. Or we could imagine chance as a diffuse energy source, one that through the mere fact of its existence has a regulating effect, as a kind of complement to our own production of order. And we might imagine that through this complement, chance, we acquire a safeguard against our own overproduction of order.

SPACES

This reminds me of something I once read about weather modeling, which involves gathering all manner of meteorological information—measurements of temperature, pressure, humidity, etc., everything the meteorologists can come up with—via a network of specific geographic points. The article described meteorologists' fondest dream: perfect measurements, using perfect instruments, so that they could predict a month ahead of time whether there would be sunshine or rain in any place on earth. The entire surface of the planet would be covered with sensors positioned at half-meter intervals, capable of gathering data from even the highest layers of the atmosphere, with all the data fed continuously into a supercomputer, so that for any day or time, right down to the minute, they could predict when and how it would rain, for instance, here in Copenhagen. But at almost the same instant that the computer began processing, tiny deviations would arise in the spaces between the sensors. At first these would create only very small errors in the computer's calculations, but the errors would quickly grow and spread, ultimately becoming global.

I noted that this phenomenon was called "the butterfly effect," a term taken from a paper by E. N. Lorenz titled "Does the Flap of a Butterfly's Wings in Brazil Set Off a Tornado in Texas?" What this hypothetical scenario may be telling us, if anything, is that the overproduction of order, or the production of absolute order, is desirable, at least for meteorologists and the weather-dependent industries they serve. But luckily the scenario is impossible, since it's impossible to create a grid the size of the whole planet. Luckily, because who would ever set foot outdoors if we were never to be surprised by a cloudburst, never to have an unexpected gust of wind sting our eyes to tears, and never able to yearn for the first really springlike day because we already knew down to the minute when it would arrive—say, on March 8th at 12:07 p.m.?

The absurdity of this kind of wishful thinking, this urge to map out, pin down, and add up, may be easier to grasp if we imagine an analogous ongoing measurement of bodily functions, tracking every minuscule movement and change in all our physical processes, until the computer suddenly started beeping away and spit out its result in the form of a message telling us when, down to the second, we would die. Better to call chance an ally, and hope to trump the computer by getting run over by a truck.

And better to have the butterfly effect. All the little spaces where chance comes in. The little spaces between our senses, the spaces between awareness and unawareness, those between words on paper, the unfathomable space of the blank page, the spaces in sleep, in formlessness, the spaces in the desolate stretches where we're outside of everything, until we're inside again. All the places where consciousness gives way to the play of chance. Better to have the butterfly effect than total order. Better to let the least little speck of randomness spread to become a sea of chance in which consciousness drowns, than to let consciousness cling to its own bounded and therefore fictive order.

FORTUNA

What's starting to look interesting here is clearly not the extent to which chance prevails, but the ways that it prevails. Nor the extent to which we're subject to the necessary order within nature, of which we're a part, but the ways that the order within nature—which human beings observe and thus compound and magnify—relates to what I call the regulating effect of chance.

Fortuna, the Roman goddess of destiny, symbolizes the arbitrariness that rules the world. She's unmoved by supplication, not because she's evil or spiteful, but because she's indifferent to the consequences of all the caprices of chance. She's pictured with a steering oar, steering the voyage of life. But she's simultaneously portrayed as a blind goddess, and over the years she came to be associated with all the previously existing goddesses of luck and happiness, so that eventually, besides the steering oar, she acquired a horn of plenty as an attribute. The whole figure presents an image of blind chance fostering fruitfulness, prosperity, and victory. As long as we understand how to navigate according to her conditions. And in terms of literature and writing, we can add: as long as we understand how to write according to those conditions.

In daily life, chance generally conceals its prima facie cruelty so well that we can play with the concept of chance. For example, we can think back over our lives and imagine how things might have been different. What if one had run away from home as a child and had never been found; what if one had been born in a completely different place, a cemetery in Cairo, maybe; what if one had become a pharmacist or a botanist, or had a church wedding with the baker's son; what if one had never gone out on that rainy winter night when one fell in love with a footloose wanderer, or if on a completely different winter night, as a different traveler, one had stepped off the train at some random stop and walked into a random house—and above all, what if one had never begun to write poetry, or to write at all.

But what's done is done. There's no denying that way back when, I did begin to write, presumably due to a chance turn of events; but that chance turn and others like it not only led me to the situation in which I'm holding forth right now, they obviously also led me to hold forth on this subject of chance itself. And so, as if it weren't enough to make a virtue of necessity, as the saying goes, they also led me to make a virtue of chance.

That's how we can play with the idea of never having begun to write. But we can also be plagued by the idea that we did begin. I've heard many writers say that it was essentially by chance that they started to write, but then suddenly one day, they had to recognize that writing had become a necessity for them. And even if that feeling of necessity may initially take writers by surprise, as a rule they don't have a very hard time believing in it and then going on to believe that the feeling of chance was just a stage that they've now moved past. For by writing, we produce order, maybe in our own lives as well, and maybe to a point where the project of living and the project of writing blend, so that writing and living no longer can be separated, but become parts of the same necessity. And that may sound like a very good thing. Almost as if it could resolve the old dilemma of integrating the course of our writing with the course of our life, by invoking a higher necessity—or destiny.

But our incessant harping on necessity may be covering up nothing more than an attempt to eliminate chance. Why? Maybe just because we want to avoid feeling as random as we are. But maybe also for more complex reasons. Maybe because of a fear of writing without any guidance from the feeling of necessity, a fear of arriving at the point where the order experienced by writers as innate and at the same time painstakingly constructed must give way, because chance has implemented an order so different that writers' hearts pound, they're frightened, and they look with complete disbelief at what they've written, which seems, even there on the page in their own handwriting, like nothing they ever could have written, simply because for all their feeling of necessity, they never would have been able to conceive of it before they started writing. A pure and simple fear of arriving at the point where chance takes their work away from them, even before they've finished writing it.

When we manage, in spite of everything, to control that fear, it can be because human beings aren't the only things with a drive to produce orderly forms. We can observe these forms everywhere in nature, and we can see how easily all kinds of matter on earth—so why not human consciousness as well?—will yield to what I'm calling the regulating effect of chance. In this way we can find comfort in imagining that it's possible to write as easily as frost creates its fernlike repetitions and variations on a windowpane, or as concisely as the flesh of a kiwifruit clings to the black cardinal points of its seeds, and even that it might be possible to write completely gray on gray, as when a large cloud, without edges or breaks, will very slowly, as it spreads, begin to reveal a consistency and a direction.

RECOGNIZABLE IMAGES

And the comfort doesn't come from thinking of these natural phenomena as direct models for how a writer should write. They're more like recognizable images of inner realities, so that what we see in the frost ferns, the kiwifruit, and the gray cloud immediately makes us exclaim, "Yes—that's what it's like to be a writer!" Or for that matter, "Yes—that's what it's like to be alive!"

Novalis keeps coming back to these images, maybe especially to their similarities, as if they all had originated long ago from one and the same writing. In his beautiful introduction to *The Novices of Sais* he says:

> Various are the roads of man. He who follows and compares them will see strange figures emerge, figures which seem to belong to that great cipher which we discern written everywhere, in wings, eggshells, clouds, and snow, in crystals and in stone formations, on ice-covered waters, on the inside and the outside of mountains, of plants, beasts, and men, in the lights of heaven … or in iron filings around a magnet, and in strange conjunctures of chance. In them we suspect a key to the magic writing, even a grammar, but our surmise takes on no definite forms and seems unwilling to become a higher key.

No, even when we suspect a key to the magic writing, it's never easy to yield to the regulating effect of chance. No matter what perspective we use, it will never be as easy to write as to breathe. Even though writers, in rare moments, can feel that it is. Can feel themselves arrive, with their fear intact, at the point in the writing process where, for lack of a better expression, they can say that chance takes over, the point where language comes to life and produces itself, in the same sense that a sunflower seed produces a sunflower. And even though it may be only an illusion, they'll swear that they actually feel writing merge with living. It's this condition of absent presence, which can be either long- or short-lived, that writers fear from the outset, because they're both afraid to attain it and afraid not to attain it. But when all is said and done, it's probably also exactly this condition that writers hope, deep in their heart, to elicit and nurture, whatever the cost and whatever other reasons there may be for writing.

So that's actually what writers struggle toward: getting this longed-for condition to happen or, more accurately, getting themselves not to stand in the way of its happening. The Viennese satirist Karl Kraus sums up the struggle precisely and paradoxically: "Es genügt nicht, keine Einfälle zu haben, man muß auch unfähig sein, sie auszudrücken." ("It's not enough to have no ideas; one must also be incapable of expressing them.")

Ironically enough, when this condition does arrive, the struggle is rewarded in an unexpected and far from gentle way. As things unfold, it becomes abundantly clear that it's no longer the writer arriving, it's chance per se, which also makes the writer random and in fact ultimately makes the just-finished manuscript random as well. In this way, chance underscores emptiness. As if what was written had never been written. As if the act of writing could result only in an increase in what has not yet been written.

Here the writer is left behind, since the work has long since slipped away from him, and he retains only the memory of a feeling that, as Novalis puts it, "seems unwilling to become a higher key." And here the excerpt from *The Novices of Sais* continues:

> It is as though an alcahest [according to Paracelsus, an *alcahest* was a universal solvent, also called *Menstruum Universale*—I.C.] had been poured over the senses of men. Only at moments do their desires and thoughts seem to solidify. Thus arise their presentiments, but after a short time everything swims again before their eyes.

So the writer is left directionless and forsaken, in something diffuse, indistinct; in something formless, random; in the exact shadow of the randomness in which he, throughout the course of his work, suspected connections. And now he must cope with a blindness, a confusion, and a feeling of loss that, with each of his attempts to transform them to plenitude, only deepen.

Eventually, after we've been through this a few times, we might expect to adjust to these bizarre conditions. After all, we know perfectly well that at the moment we put pen to paper, the text is completely unpredictable, whereas at the other end of the process, when it's finally written, it will seem very predictable.

As the text is being written, it comes to seem more and more necessary, as it gradually develops rules, proportion, and order, while the finished text, laid out in final form, will appear random. Because it's not until afterward, when the text is finished, that we can say with certainty that it could just as easily have been different. And to the degree that it could have been different, to that degree it is random.

Everything that a writer writes could just as easily have been different—but not until it's been written. As a life could have been different, but not until it's been lived.

THE AMORPHOUS

So why put ourselves through it all again and again, only to achieve an ever-deepening feeling of loss? Of course it would be understandable to want to live our lives over again. But why put ourselves through any of the more possible things again, like writing, for example? Why attempt by that means to achieve something that in reality is impossible to achieve; why get into a game in which, despite exceptional opportunities, there is only one possible end result: you're out.

Maybe because it's about a particular kind of intoxication of our consciousness, the feeling of ascending into formlessness without its really happening, the feeling of finding ourselves a part of the amorphous without needing to die; in fact, if religion didn't hold a patent on God, including linguistically, I'd call it the feeling of being clay in God's hands, as when giving birth and perhaps also when being born—always in situations where there is an apparent absence of differentiation between the body and its surroundings.

And here we must not think of the amorphous as exclusively

undifferentiated and immovable. Rather, we might conceive of it as a place of origin, unknown, nondescript, as long ago, when light broke and called forth the first microscopic independent movement in matter, still far from the complex organic forms we know today, and further yet from our indefatigable descriptions of them, and from these descriptions' colder abstractions, such as geometry. Mandelbrot asks, "Why is geometry often seen as 'cold' and 'dry'?" and goes on to posit an answer:

> One reason lies in its inability to describe the shape of a cloud, a mountain, a coastline, or a tree. Clouds are not spheres, mountains are not cones, coastlines are not circles, and bark is not smooth, nor does lightning travel in a straight line.... The existence of these patterns challenges us to study those forms that Euclid sets aside as being "formless," to investigate the morphology of the "amorphous."

We'll have to leave the direct study of the amorphous to fractal geometry. But we can still think about our own urge to seek out situations that resemble what we could call the amorphous. In intoxication, maybe; in love's meeting; in the city's stream of anonymous people; in a tropical climate; in the warmth of the body; here and in similar fascinations, from time to time we can experience an approximation to the amorphous, to an absence of differentiation, to being outside the world. But only an approximation. Any more would kill us. Experiencing a perceptible lack of differentiation between skin and air, between body and world, between human being and human being is idyllic, almost Edenic, but taken to its logical conclusion it would mean death: simply put, the eradication of the individual. This is no doubt the reason that we all long to see this experience simulated in art, and the reason that writers attempt to achieve a linguistic Eden, a paradise in which writer and language merge, even though time after time, the writer ends up banished from the very paradise that he feels that he, all on his own, has created.

So it looks as if the writer's drive to connect with the regulating effect of chance may—as it relates to our consciousness of our own and others' mortality—also relate to our concept of paradise, a Garden of Eden, a mystical place where human beings exist undifferentiated from the world.

The word *paradise* comes from Avestan, the language of ancient Persia, where it meant "a bounded, enclosed garden." Outside this garden lies the desert of sand, where life has no possibilities. However, if the desert did not exist as an "anti-garden" (a term coined by Lebanese poet Salah Stétié in his *Firdaws*)—then the garden would not exist either, because it is defined by its boundary with the desert. Occasionally people in that part of the world used to go out into the desert for days and immerse themselves in prayer. Perhaps to become able to perceive garden and anti-garden as parts of the same secret.

Back then, paradise and voluntary exile from paradise were still very real and everyday, but our concepts of the mystical gardens framing all of humanity's life are not so very different from these first experiences of the relationship between an ordinary garden and an ordinary desert. They're just played out on a grander scale, in which they become fictive, but not necessarily any less real for our purposes.

Our mythological constructs include two gardens. One is the Garden of Eden, the first paradise, God's earthly garden, where the first human beings were happy because they didn't know that they were alive. And the other is a second paradise, human beings' heavenly garden, where we will be happy some day because we won't know that we're dead. The first paradise, where human existence was part of nature, and the last, where human beings will be part of the same numinous light that created the first, exist in the same relationship to each other as the garden to the anti-garden, as the oasis to the desert, and, in the final analysis, as life to death.

When Adam and Eve were banished from the first garden, from paradise, it happened because they had eaten the fruit of the Tree of Knowledge and had thus become witnesses to the world and to their own life.

And maybe, in the process, had caught a hint of the regulating effect of chance. As they stood outside, with that hint as their only possession, there in the desert, they became witnesses not only to their life but also to the irreversible character of that life. And there on the spot they were forced to transform their immediate longing to return to paradise into a longing to move forward, a longing, greater than anything else in the world, to recreate the missing paradise, preferably of course before dying, but afterward if necessary, in a transfiguring light on which we, with perhaps better reason than we think, pin our faith that we have been part of it since the dawn of time and will therefore remain so until time ends.

So we are banished, and at the same time obliged to live for an unknowable length of time with a longing for the first garden, which resembles the gardens of our childhood, and with a lack of longing, or at least an ambivalent longing, for the second garden, which, if we aren't convinced of its literal existence, starts to resemble a cemetery. Garden and anti-garden, which can never become one, and which can be conceived of as one only in abstract visions.

There is no doubt that our concepts of paradise express the fact that we as human beings are not only able to imagine a condition of ongoing want, but are also able to maintain this condition of want and moreover to call it life, as for example in literature, where writers repeatedly approach it in order to subdue it, but end up each time with a deeper sense of loss, more homeless and more firmly banished with every attempt.

One could get the idea that we actually invented paradise in order to become homeless—and to remain homeless, since a paradise after death may not be a particularly tempting offer. So we prefer to seek out a paradise that we can continue to lose, time and again, so that our conversation about what we've lost, and about our feeling of unconditional want, can continue.

About this conversation: maybe we could try altering the terms of what we call paradise. If paradise is not only missing, but also in an absolute sense nonexistent—because it's not even we who will enter paradise, but only the dust that all of us, without exception, will some day become—then maybe, just by thinking differently, we could give paradise a new address.

ANAGRAM

I have an anagram that might be useful here. If we take the Italian word for paradise—*paradiso*—and rearrange the letters, we get *diaspora*. *Diaspora* is the Greek word for "scattering" or "diffusion." It can be used to refer to religious groups or believers in any set of ideas, who live, or are forced to live, dispersed in lands where beliefs are different from their own. One example is the Jewish people sometimes called Diaspora Jews.

A whole new exercise could be inherent in this anagram, one that might slowly shift the address of paradise. All we have to do, each time we read the word *paradise*, is act as if we have become dyslexic enough to see it as *diaspora*. It's true that we're banished from paradise, but maybe we've brought it along, literally, in our diaspora. And considering how European history is going these days, it may not be such a bad idea for us to become able to see our diaspora as a mystical place of human beings' undifferentiated existence in the world.

FRAGMENTS AND ROUNDABOUT ROUTES

Among Leonardo da Vinci's notes is a set of precepts for painters. They appear in a separate section of the *Treatise on Painting*, which we know was put into book form not by Leonardo himself but most likely by his close friend and student, Francesco Melzi. This section appears to include everything that wouldn't quite fit in with the more practical advice in the other chapters, which consist primarily of detailed instructions for painting monsters, storms, night scenes, trees and smaller plants, morning sunlight, late afternoon sunlight, etc. etc. The various notes that couldn't be included with those practical instructions are largely theoretical artistic considerations concerning artists' relationship to their material as a whole, and the issue of beginning any specific work of art. For example:

> I cannot forbear to mention among these precepts a new device for study, which, although it may seem but trivial and almost ludicrous, is nevertheless exceedingly useful in arousing the mind to various inventions. And this is, when you look at a wall spotted with stains, or with a mixture of stones, if you have to devise some scene, you may discover a resemblance to various landscapes, beautified with mountains, rivers, rocks, trees, plains, wide valleys, and hills in varied arrangement; or again you may see battles and figures in action; or strange faces and costumes, and an endless variety of objects, which you could reduce to complete and well-drawn forms. And these appear on such walls confusedly, like the sound of bells in whose jangle you may find any name or word you choose to imagine.

Here Leonardo da Vinci, in all innocence, says that random stains and similar things "arouse the mind to inventions." And that may be all that's needed: given enough fragments, the human brain may immediately start to organize and regulate and create meaning in anything at all.

In what sense might Leonardo's stained walls, or the wall outside my kitchen window, cobbled together using discarded bricks of various colors from periods of hasty industrialization during previous centuries, be this kind of fragment? It's their history that marks the discolored yellowish, grayish, and reddish discarded bricks, once remnants of some construction or demolition project, as fragments, reused parts of an earlier whole. And their history also marks the possibility that the current whole may disintegrate, so that they might eventually become part of a different context, as yet unknown. But their journey from grand edifice to grand edifice, or from grand edifice to humble prefabricated house and maybe at last to some chance rubble pile dumped in a field—if we can see this journey only as a set of roundabout routes subordinate to various wholes, then we'll never be able to see the fragments as things in themselves, detached from everything else; we'll have to settle for seeing them as forgotten, remembered, or foreseen parts of a whole from which we can detach neither the bricks nor ourselves. Could it be that no matter what fragments we encounter, along the lines of the random stains on Leonardo's walls, we're not only able but actually forced to have them arouse our minds to invention? In other words, does our mental makeup condemn us to find meaning even where there is none? Or as Jean-François Lyotard phrases the question, "Why does something happen, instead of nothing?"

EDENKOBEN

I'd like to turn for a moment to the enduring ways of depicting paradise. The first paradise, the Garden of Eden, is always subtropical. A lush garden with palm trees, grapevines, etc. A continuous profusion of abundant nourishment. Always set in countries with subtropical climates, this illusion of happiness.

Last fall I visited the German town of Edenkoben, in Rheinland-Pfalz. It's not subtropical. But even in the fall, and even without palm trees, the illusion of paradise is perfect, at least for someone from northern lands. The name alone: Edenkoben. I ask people what Edenkoben means. No one knows. Edenkoben is just Edenkoben in Rheinland-Pfalz. Vineyards everywhere. Everywhere the exacting process of preparing intoxication. So why ask what Edenkoben means, any more than we would ask why we're alive.

The window in my room, with its broad view over the rolling

landscape, shows a modern image of paradise. Model towns like those on Christmas cards. Factories that seem to sail like old-fashioned ships through forest seas. And although they're undoubtedly polluting and ruining everything for miles around, you think you can hear the rustling of the Tree of Knowledge of Good and Evil. Even though you know that it must be only the tree of recognition.

One morning the window and the whole landscape, including the house, are swathed in a kind of cloud, in something unconditional and unreserved, a kind of primordial soup. Thousands of birds, starlings, I think at first—but they're not metallic black like starlings, maybe redwing thrushes, which I've seen only once in my life, a small flock in Jutland, so I'm not really familiar with them, these birds, which I'm now thinking of as redwing thrushes—fill the air over Edenkoben and make it into a kind of earth. Grapevines and thrushes become one cohesive phenomenon. Earth and air are no longer two separate elements, but one, as when all becomes one. So where shall we breathe? Where shall we die? Where shall we even ask questions?

That morning I look through the postcards I've brought with me. They include one with Goethe's *aquarellierte Federzeichnung: Farbenkreis zur Symbolisierung des menschlichen Geistes- und Seelenlebens* (pen-and-ink drawing with watercolor: colored circles to symbolize the life of the human spirit and soul); one with a pen-and-ink sketch by Hans Christian Andersen, of cypresses in an Italian landscape; and one with a photograph of a mummy from the Egyptian Museum in Berlin. All three are actually fragments of paradise. Maybe especially the mummy: a woman who has already been dead for 2,500 years, and who can be seen now only because part of her coffin has been lifted off. The lid over her bears her portrait carved in wood, probably more regular in form than her real face, just as the hair is probably blacker and the makeup more precise; at any rate the smile is more enigmatic than the usual dead person's smile. Maybe the painter knew how long people have to wait to enter paradise.

These more or less idyllic musings are interrupted when small automatic rockets suddenly begin going off in the vineyard in front of the house, with loud bangs and flashing sparks, to scare away the birds. The birds fly around for a bit, making the air currents over the landscape visible. Then all at once they're gone, and paradise looks completely desolate and forsaken.

The redwing thrushes should have been birds of paradise. The bird of paradise family, related to swallows, includes 32 genera and 129 species. They're native to New Guinea and the surrounding islands. Europeans first learned of birds of paradise after Magellan's voyage around the world. From that trip, in 1522, he brought back stuffed birds of paradise. Their beauty and unusual appearance awakened great wonder. They were given the name *Manucodiata*, which means "birds of God," and soon countless stories about them began circulating. People claimed, among other things, that the birds lived in heaven, and that their feet were missing because they spent their entire lives in the air, existing on dew. It was true that their feet were missing, but that was just because the hunters who gave the dead birds to Magellan had cut off the feet to make the carcasses look more beautiful. This was neither the first nor the last time that fragmentation has been turned into a beautiful explanation.

Around noon I visit the *Altdeutsche Weinstube* in Edenkoben. Nine tables, including the one for regulars, where a group of workmen sits. An old man walking around seeing to everything quietly and calmly, as if all the guests were his own family, who may make things a little difficult now and then, in their way, but they're here now, and they've come to stay.

"May I see a menu?" I ask.

"Here you eat what's being served," he says, echoing the words of my mother when I was a child: "Here you eat what's put in front of you." The others at the table nod. There's no reason to discuss the food. And they're right: it's always good.

Later, after everyone has finished and the old man himself has eaten, I ask him what Edenkoben means.

It means nothing, he says, nothing at all. Then he adds, "But *Eden* means 'Eden,' like the Garden of Eden. And *Koben* is the old word for 'stable.' Stable," he repeats. "This restaurant is like a stable. The people who come here are like horses; they can't go any farther without food and drink. But why go any farther anyhow." And he looks as if he's found his own way to cope with a world where much is missing.

A world where paradise is missing, but now and then we find a stable that lets us remember what is missing. A place where we're strangers, yet at home, where we're alone, yet together. A place where we're nothing, yet still something. Dust, yet still, for a while, human beings. But fundamentally it remains a place that tells us paradise is missing, because it is not we who will enter paradise; it is dust. Dust, because it is undifferentiated enough to assume a form of existence outside the world.

TO ACT AS IF

Of course, as long as we're alive, we'll never become so fragmentary that we're able to exist outside the world. But is it possible, amid the productions of our consciousness, to imagine a fragmentary existence? Are we at least able to think our way out of the world we live in?

Don't we tend to see a literary fragment, for example, as a concentrated text whose concentration stems from the hidden whole that it's a part of? Or we see the opposite: we see the fragment as trying to distance itself from the hidden whole, from the development of any whole at all. Regardless, it doesn't manage to establish any relationships that aren't involved with a whole in one way or another. Maurice Blanchot, in his *L'entretien infini*, renders this issue as a postulate: "Le fragmentaire ne précède pas le tout, mais se dit en dehors du tout et après lui." (The fragmentary does not precede the whole, but says itself *outside* the whole and after it.)

We should probably always expect a postulate to be an impossible blend of question and answer. For of course we can't say anything outside the whole or after it, as long as we're inside it. But are there any roundabout routes that would let us escape not only the order built into our nature and culture, but also its remnants in any fragment we run across? Or at least, is it possible for us to act as if we can see ourselves from outside, and to say or write something that's outside everything and after everything?

Of course it's possible to act as if. We definitely have as part of our intellect, for better or for worse, the strange ability to act as if things are completely different from what they are—or from what we see them as. A burning bush can speak, the Spirit of God can move upon the face of the waters, a little prince can run around on a planet that he himself has discovered, a whole country can be populated by talking trees, and there's nothing to hinder dust from talking too: all these manipulative, seductive productions are familiar from literature, and not only from literature, because they're also familiar from our daily social interactions. However, there the seduction tends in large part to develop into demagoguery, fairly harmless as a rule, because it's easy to see through. But occasionally it becomes chillingly harmful, as when we find that some people are able to convince themselves that the concentration camps of World War II never existed, and we see that it might not take much more for these people's story to erase every trace, if in no other way than by wiping out the remnants of shared memory that we're trying to maintain.

In a way, I think we should try to live with a reduction of meaning. To get rid of the idea that there is any meaning beyond what we've always been able to recognize, to reflect, and to simulate—an ability stemming from our existence as precisely that part of meaning that's able to see its own meaning—no more, no less. Applied to literature, this would still let a writer do things like using a distant planet as a vantage point to observe the teeming of life on earth, but his description would never give it any meaning beyond the meaning that it already has on earth. Would writers stop writing because of that? Probably not. Just as scientists don't stop pondering relationships among phenomena, but ultimately must accept that the earth is held in place by what we call gravity, even though they would prefer a different, more comprehensive explanation, which they can only entrust, for the time being, to meaninglessness.

It's nothing new for art and science to operate at the boundary between meaning and meaninglessness. But the boundary may be more fluid than we generally believe. Many things suggest that it's no longer unequivocally what it once was: a boundary that progress is forcing ever further forward, into the unknown, the open and boundless realm of possibility. It's more as if the boundary has shifted into the middle of our closed system. And here, for the first time, paradise truly has become lost. We could call it paradise re-lost. With the result that we have to begin dreaming our way inward, instead of forward or back.

THE FROG IN THE SPACESHIP

It's hard to imagine how we might dream our way inward. We're so used to dreaming our way outward, away from our little life, out toward distant horizons, whether on the other side of the earth or far off in other nebulae where there may be other planets that could support human existence.

As a small attempt to dream my way inward, I might picture myself living inside a sunflower seed, as an entirely miniaturized human essence in there, a sunflower creature, looking up toward a sky that may be black in my mind now, as I think about it from out here, but from in there—who knows, maybe it is white or a dazzling spectrum of colors—I might picture myself conceptually unable to get out of the seed or move upward, it would be impossible: with no idea that it could be possible to rise with the stem, as it sprouted leaves and a big round flower with flame-shaped yellow petals, like a corona around the sun-core with its new seeds, much less with any idea that this sunflower with its core and corona would turn, day by day, tilting, seeking, the heavy sun-head following a sun incomprehensibly larger than itself. And it's fine that I can picture things like that. But how, or in relationship to what, my mental pictures are outside or inside the world—I'm beginning to question whether that ultimately makes any difference.

As I began writing this, I read in the *Neue Kronen Zeitung* (September, 1992) that an American space shuttle had been launched with seven astronauts on board. The shuttle was to orbit the earth for seven days, almost like a symbolic week of creation, with the seven astronauts devoting their time to scientific studies. They were going to conduct biology experiments with four frogs, one hundred eighty hornets, two carp, and two hundred fruit flies. I don't know the results. But later, as I watched on TV, a smiling Japanese astronaut amid the space shuttle's vast array of instruments and equipment was trying to get one of the four frogs to jump normally despite the absence of gravity. To no avail. The frog would only float belly up, legs splayed out on all sides, like a bloated corpse. In a way the scene began to look like a random fragment from Noah's Ark. A little pilot project for our diffuse strivings to move beyond the earth. As if, basically, we just wanted to get out of this solar system in time, before our sun burns out, and land on any other planet that's even remotely habitable, as long as it's orbiting a sun longer-lived than our own.

All the confusion and uncertainty around that fragment, and around our own fragmented position and its shift relative to the world around us, is magnified by our ambivalent attitude toward the relationship between nature and culture; that is, between nature and what is created by human beings. In one way we have a primitive longing to get back to nature, a sentimental nostalgia, whereas in another way we have eyes for absolutely nothing but the man-made world around us. And that man-made world is certainly taking up so much room now that it's starting to scare even us. But instead of investigating the intimate relationships between the productions of human beings and those of nature—from which we do, after all, originate—we often regard nature and the man-made world as two separate entities, irreconcilable and even inimical to each other.

FANTASY IMAGES

The grotesqueness of a purely man-made world becomes evident in these fantasy images from *The Painted Room*, a novel I wrote in the 1970s about the artist Andrea Mantegna, who lived in Mantua in the late 1400s. In this passage, Mantegna's ten-year-old son Bernardino describes the landscape he imagines exploring whenever he looks at a certain painting by his father. What becomes clear before his astonished eyes is the relationship between nature and artifice, or the frightening aspect of artifice.

> I set out right away. It is peaceful and green on all sides and I climb up toward the high town with great expectation. But I am not very high up before I realize something or other is different, something that cannot be made out because I have never seen it before. Now I come to the forked tree and climb up and sit in it: I have to find out what is wrong. But I cannot see anything. The trees are all the usual trees I know so well; the houses are houses like those in Mantua or like those the architects draw or like the ones we found in the spring when the school was out on a dig; the fields are green, the sky is blue, and the rocks have the usual brownish, bluish or greenish colors; even the tiny people,

whom I hope to meet, look completely natural. Yet I cannot get away from the thought that something is wrong. The atmosphere is wrong, as when you kill a chicken and it runs around without its head.

I climb down and move on. When I am up the road over the largest quarry, I stop. At this point I have already passed quite a few smaller quarries and underground shafts, but it is not until I reach this place close to the rocks and have a view of the whole area where the stonemasons have worked their way into the wonderful marble, that I realize what it is that is different:

The mountain has been made by people. Not only the town up on the very top, with its walls and forts and everything which is normally built by people, but the whole enormous mountain that lifts the town up into the light, it is all made by people, from the ground up, foot by foot, so the stones look almost real, they almost have the same odd shapes, almost the same sheen as real stone, or natural stone.

It is beyond me. Have these stonemasons' forefathers taken thousands of years to build up this mountain, only for their descendants to open it up and mine the stone again?

And where did they get the stone from? Did they fetch it from another place? Or did they also make the stone themselves? If the stone we usually call stone is the real stone, then this stone is not real and natural or divine. The stone I am now touching is a human stone. At one time there were people, here on this spot, who not only produced the mountain, but also produced the stone that the mountain is made of.

I walk up to the red gate-tower to ask to go in past the sloping wall between the captain's fortress and the city wall itself. To the left of the tower a ruin has been built with short columns and low arches of rough-hewn stones. I do not think the rest of this building has ever existed. I am sure it was built as a ruin by people who knew that ruins should remind them of something, but did not know what they should remind them of. To the right there is a steep slope planted with trees, with five or six large blocks of marble, columns, pyramids, and vats, all made of the same man-made marble as what I am walking on. It occurs to me that these people must have known what is needed to create history, but they have forgotten the history itself, or never had any idea about its existence.

A vision of human beings as manipulators of layer upon layer of fragments, whose origins have long since been forgotten. A caricature of human beings' ability to convince themselves that everything they've invented and placed in the world is just as unique and magnificent as what nature has developed on its own. A basic insistence that history belongs to us, even though we have forgotten the foundation that it's built on. And although we may be able to see perfectly well that Mt. Everest, the Alps, and all the rest came into being without human assistance, still it's not beyond us to think that if they ever disappeared, and we wanted them to exist again, then it would be within our power to reinvent and rebuild them; in fact, that we could create the originals themselves just as well as any god could. This arrogance arises because for so long we've been setting up our human world as if it were the whole world, as if our human takeover of nature would take the old-fashioned longing for paradise and transform it to eternal security in an artificial paradise. And now that we're living in that artificial paradise, at least in certain parts of the planet, we realize that we've cut ourselves off from nature, rather than bringing it along into our world and managing it. We've actually done the furthest thing from bringing it along: we've made our culture dependent on power sources, like nuclear fission and fusion, which function in a natural cycle entirely different from the one we function in as human beings—if we can say that radioactive materials function in any type of cycle related to what we know as nature. Their half-lives, which are the lengths of time that they can poison us, range from around one hundred to one thousand years. Instead of supplementing human energy with these antihuman substances, we should be keeping ourselves warm by taking the most roundabout possible route to the goal, creating images of a more symbiotic relationship with nature, which we do certainly need to control, but not to such a degree that we become victims of our control.

THE TRIUMPH OF VANITY

What's important, maybe, is to avoid creating sharp divisions between nature and human culture, and instead to try seeing our own productions more as part of a natural process. Here again I want to use an excerpt from *The Painted Room*, this time a description of Mantegna's approach to establishing himself in the world and building a house, as told by an initially disconcerted but later admiring and perceptive administrator attached to the Ducal court.

It is very likely that the house will never be finished.

The plan has been to have an arched dome over the atrium, but Andrea has at last given up that project and instead let someone carve a marble basin to collect rainwater and snow.

Of the fifteen rooms, only a couple are completed with walls and doors. The housekeeper lives in one of the rooms. And the other, for the most part, is left empty. In the rest of the house there are only hints where one has to imagine boundaries for the individual rooms, sometimes with unfinished brickwork, sometimes with a pair of columns, but in most cases, with a pile of sculptures, antiques, and plants.

The plants grow almost better here indoors than outside. During the summer they press their way in through the outer wall of the garden unrestrictedly, seeking shade and coolness from the whitewashed room.

All the same, Mantegna works tirelessly on this artistic building and spends all of what he owns on marble, on color samples, on firing and glazing, on fusing and chasing, and on the cleverest and most expressive artisans. This patience costs him dear.

I am not saying that I hope the house is never finished. I am not saying that, but deep down, it is exactly what I hope for. I am attracted to the ill-defined transitions between Art and Nature, and when I see the way the young apprentices who come here to learn drawing and perspective fare better in depicting the leafy vines that wind around the base of a column than they do with the column itself, then I am deeply delighted. And if I see them mistake flowers and fruit for different sorts of colored stones, I am more delighted than ever. Then I see how strong the physical world is when it reveals itself obliquely to artists' educated perceptions.

It's starting to look like the dream is about building a ruin in advance. About setting up a paradise we can't lose, because it's lost from the start. About seeing a paradise in any diaspora at all. As if it could be possible to delay irreversible time, put off the inevitable, by setting up images of the triumph of the transitory, of vanity, in everyday life.

THE DOMAIN OF CONTINGENCY

In this everyday life, we live in a domain of contingency. Here nothing in existence relates exclusively to itself. Here everything always relates to something else, and on and on. The apple is green, we say, but there would be no need to call the apple green if the apple were the only green thing in the world. The apple is green only because in the domain of contingency so many other green things exist that we're forced to invent the word *green* to keep ourselves oriented— in other words, to show comparisons.

In the same way, the apple is round like all the other round things in our experience: the moon, the earth, the sun. And not even the sun—which otherwise serves so much as a point of reference in the domain of contingency—not even the sun has roundness to itself;

even the sun is round only by comparison to everything else that's round: apples, pupils of eyes, jellyfish, etc.

Because of this, in the domain of contingency there are only roundabout routes. Endless motion from green to green, from round to round, etc., that can never provide a full overview of roundness itself, for example, or greenness.

Yet we humans are put together in such a way that we would lay down our very lives to bring all that motion to a temporary standstill, so that we could get a comprehensive view of those unsettling roundabout routes. This tends not to work out so well for people who do come close to the truth. It works out better for people who, in response to whatever specific truth they think is coming close, gather up so much data that the truth moves further away again. Ultimately, of course, that just makes life in the domain of contingency richer.

Occasionally we hear that history is at an end. But maybe it's only moving into a new domain. Maybe we can pleat history back onto itself to see whether, in its labyrinthine passages, there are repetitions suggesting that even history unfolds in terms of contingency. If that is the case, then not only will it have to be rewritten, but the rewriting will have to be continuous. This means that history can never come to an end. History itself will enter, once and for all, into the domain of contingency.

(1994)

I Think, Therefore I Am Part of the Labyrinth

Baroque refers to the period from 1600 to 1700, or, in all time periods, to a thing that doesn't reveal its overarching similarities until it has overwhelmed us with differences. In Portuguese, *il barocco* means an irregular pearl. And the Baroque is just such an irregular pearl: a magnificent, odd, preposterous, downright tasteless distorted pearl, not at all perfect, but perfectly different.

Or rather: it's not satisfied with being perfect; it also wants to reveal perfection as an irregularity in the way people create their concepts of the world.

On one of the first days of the year 1600, Giordano Bruno is burned at the stake because he believes in more than one concept of the world. He believes in Christianity among people, and between people and God, and he believes that there are many worlds in the universe. He himself is not troubled by this, delighting in these contradictory and apparently irreconcilable concepts. But the medieval guardians of perfection consider it madness if things don't all fit into the same order. And Bruno is burned at the stake.

At the same time, Shakespeare is writing about Hamlet, about how the world order Prince Hamlet lives in has collapsed, and how he has to feign madness to conceal that he has perceived that collapse.

This play, about which of those two conditions is madness, is running everywhere, in winter or spring. In reality it's the time of all seasons; but parents are devouring their own children in an attempt to get the world to stand still, so they can keep up and forget that they themselves are the ones who have to die.

Bonfires are burning everywhere in Europe, and the spectators are streaming out to rejoice and to learn from their rejoicing.

Those in power put on *their* latest play, and the spectators assent to it. This play has power over their minds. The spectators themselves have no power; their contribution to power is the malice they can produce.

As long as they assent to one another's joy at the violence striking the individual, they are demonstrating that they have no intention of conducting themselves as individuals.

Oppression is a bargain that most people accept because it's their only safe hiding place.

On one of the first days of the century, then, a bonfire is burning in the Piazza del Campo de' Fiori in Rome. The man dying in the flames is Giordano Bruno. He stands naked, chained to an iron post; his mouth is gagged.

If he had been able to call out to the spectators, he undoubtedly would have tried once more to get them to delight in the universe, in the thought that the earth orbits the sun; and not only that, he would have spoken to them of the fixed stars as an infinite number of suns, each surrounded by its own solar system.

Who knows, maybe it could have consoled the oppressed people to hear that they had fellow sufferers in distant worlds.

Or rather: it could have incited them to rebellion to hear and believe that "the play" that those in power had assigned them to go along with was the wrong one. Wrong, not because it didn't really exist, but because it wasn't the only right one.

That another play, another world order existed, or several, and somewhere in there perhaps a few in which they themselves could have a say in the action.

That there might even exist a world where an infinite number of people had power, simply by virtue of moving along in the right way.

That justice on earth may have consisted in something as simple as moving along in the right way, in a kind of human imitation of the fixed stars' and planets' way of moving.

Before Bruno's mouth was closed, he'd managed to formulate the following, among other things, and write it down in a dialogue with himself: "Continue to further our recognition of what, in truth, the heavens, the planets, and stars are, of how each of these infinitely many worlds is different from each other, of how it is, in infinite space, not only possible but also necessary that an infinite cause has an infinite result. Teach us what true substance, material, and creation are, who is the creator of it all, how each sentient creature is composed of the same elements and beginnings! Convince us of the doctrine of this infinite cosmos! Destroy those delusional vaults and crystalline spheres said to encompass so and so many heavens and elements! Throw open the portal, so that we can gaze out upon the immense starry universe."

Bruno wrote that in a dialogue with himself. Who read it? Of Europe's fifty million inhabitants, eighty percent were illiterate.

Only a few decades later, in the 1660s, the Danish noblewoman Leonora Christina, imprisoned in Copenhagen's Blue Tower, writes of her female guard:

> I made offer to instruct her in Reading, were she but to secure an ABC. At that she laughed scornfully and said, "Folk would think that I were daft, that I now would learn to read." I made to persuade her with Raison, to have a Pastime to while away the Hours withal, but she would have none of it: for she did know already, all that of which she had Need.

Most people were sure they knew everything they needed to know. It often felt like more than enough. And those who knew more, or knew better, were persecuted, and unhappy because knowledge without possibility of acting on that knowledge engenders insanity.

"O God! I could be bounded in a nutshell, and count myself a king of infinite space, were it not that I have bad dreams," says Hamlet.

People have always built up their concept of the world around their own consciousness, in much the same way that an oyster builds up a pearl around a grain of sand.

In the Middle Ages all people participated in singling out one and the same perfect pearl, and consciousness was firmly enclosed within the holy dome of the church and all its crystalline heavens, as if within a nutshell.

In the Renaissance more and more people shifted their consciousness out of that system. Grains of sand and foreign bodies were floating around freely, and the pearl that was built up then was the human body, the divine human, prepared to swallow God and install itself within the void as king of infinite space.

The Baroque was forced to exist in both places at once and thus found itself betwixt and between, in the abyss with bad dreams. Caught between these two giant oyster shells, the image of the world took on the form of an irregular pearl, and people survived, with a kind of fictive value intact, only by taking up residence in the vertigo and regarding existence as a kind of conjured chaos.

It looked more like nothingness. The heavens were not heavens but a void, and humans were not reborn but left to their own devices.

For now, when the universe had lifted the veil covering its infinite riches and mirror effects, it also had to speak when spoken to.

When humans had lost their identity in God, the universe had to compensate them with as many identities as there are stars in the sky.

These theatrical visions gradually changed the whole European world into a stage on which the gap between fiction and reality was obliterated as far as the masses were concerned. They were never anything but stagehands and set pieces; even as the audience they were set pieces, and in broader format they were soldiers, vagabonds, and witches—all sorts of victims of the violent grinding of the stage mechanisms.

With the witch hunts an actual drop in population could be detected. A law professor in Leipzig, Benedikt Carpzow, congratulated himself for having signed twenty thousand death warrants, the highest number in all the witch trials.

For the more economically refined, the gap between reality and fiction became a permanent stopping place, where people practiced forgetting that the basic steps of existence—its masks and hidden ambitions—could reveal themselves in the bloodiest seriousness.

Saint-Simon tells, in his memoirs from the close of the century, about the masked ball at the court of the Sun King, where wax masks of the courtiers had been created. These masks were completely true to life, and at the ball they were worn beneath the conventional masks.

At the moment when the masks were dropped, everyone thought that it was people's real faces that became visible. But in reality it was the wax masks, and the person beneath each one was someone completely different.

At the moment of truth, truth shows itself to be a true-to-life lie.

Nature, the universe if we will, had thrown people a curve by being different, and in all childishness people were trying to live up to the adult world and its inexplicable rules.

In 1605 Cervantes sends his knight Don Quixote forth to take the world's lies at their word. He will let words create what they name, recreate reality as fiction, which means recreating the world around his own mind.

So he sallies forth with his pasteboard helmet and his rusty weapons, which he believes to be a wonderful arsenal, and the public gives him a glowing welcome. Laughter bubbles up around these absurd illusions, the same laughter that a century later boils over on the occasion of the burial of Louis XIV. Stones were thrown at his coffin, bonfires were lit in the streets, so that people could dimly begin to glimpse the path toward revolution.

One evening in May of 1968 I stood in a deserted and dark street in Paris. The streetlights were almost hidden by trees in full leaf. A man came hurrying by and asked in passing, "C'est par là, la révolution?"

as he eagerly pointed in the direction he was going. "Is this the way to the revolution?" I didn't have a chance to answer, and now in 1978, I'm reminding myself that the word *révolution* in French literally means "a circular motion by means of which a moving body returns to its original position." For example, the revolution of a planet.

If the moving body is a human, I would add that it returns to its original position, but changed, always changed.

For that matter, why wouldn't that be true of planets as well? They return changed. We have not yet arrived at an understanding of the justice of the motions of the planets. Regarding human courses of motion we still behave as if the world were flat.

Kepler published his two first laws of planetary motion in 1609. It had already been quite a while since the world was flat. But even if Kepler's laws had been completely unknown, and even if people had known nothing and pursued nothing but hearsay, they already quite literally felt as if they no longer had solid ground beneath their feet.

Still, if the world itself couldn't be firm, at least one could make a model world that had the desired firmness. The world became a stage where people of all kinds, pressured by the fear of losing either their power or their lives, had to act according to specific stage directions.

The ceremonies on the occasion of the wedding of Leopold I in Vienna were on the surface an appealing demonstration of the magic of power. It was as if all the elements had been called forth, but in reality it was all the royal subjects, dressed as elements. If you retreat at my bidding, then the waters will also retreat, and the world will stay firm.

The festivities lasted for more than a year, and "the great equestrian ball" in 1667 was the pinnacle of the ceremonies. Here, whole regiments of cavalry performed, horses and riders clad in all sorts of costly finery, to illustrate the four elements: air, fire, earth, and water.

From a contemporary account:

> The elements now take up ceremonial positions, cast themselves into violent dispute, and at a whole new flourish of trumpets,

draw their weapons. In the form of an equestrian ballet in elaborate formations they conduct various skirmishes, without any victories being won. At the height of the hostilities, a dazzling light suddenly radiates above the forces and a voice commands, "Halt in the heat of battle!"

After this all the equestrians stand as if enchanted ... and behold, at the same moment the clouds part and completely unexpectedly, the Temple of Immortality floats down over the skirmishing elements, and the emperor is revealed in the doorway of the temple, mounted on horseback. He rides around the entire arena and halts before his bride to make obeisance. To conclude, the emperor conducts yet another mighty equestrian ballet!

It is really the absolute monarchy ruling the elements of the people by disciplining their fury, so that they think they're protected from all forms of rage.

But in the great theaters of the world—where the palaces naturally functioned as hugely proportioned set pieces—the rage was real and lethal enough.

Mass executions were orchestrated and presented as works of art, the condemned were led in procession, barefoot and in penitents' gowns with pointed hoods, and if any of the condemned had fled, their portraits were carried in the procession, and if they had died, their coffins were carried, and all the coffins, portraits, and barefoot penitents were executed en masse.

That kind of performance was even subject to a kind of ceremonial critique. It's reported that the mass executions carried out in Madrid in 1680 were the most "successful" that had ever taken place.

A similar kind of performance was put on in Copenhagen in 1663. Leonora Christina describes, from her jail cell in the Blue Tower, the theater of cruelty in which she lived:

Some time after the Departure of the Imperial Elector's eldest Son, it was decided that a Wood Carving would be executed [i.e., a carving of Leonora Christina's husband, Corfitz Ulfeldt], and thus in the Morning my lower Chamber was unlocked, well swept out, cleaned, and strewn with Sand. At Midday it was opened and the Woman, having on the Stairway spoken with the Coachman, came in, approached my Bed, appeared abashed and said quickly, "O Jesus, my Lady! They are bringing in Your Husband!" These Tidings terrified me, as she could easily mark; for when she pronounced them, I rose up in my Bed and stretched out my right Arm and Hand and could not manage to withdraw them again. At that she perchance felt Remorse, for I remained thus and spoke not a Word, whereupon she said, "My Lady, it is but a Carving of Your Husband." Thereupon said I, "God punish you!" She declared that I spoke with an evil Tongue, that I, not she, deserved Punishment, and she used many offensive Words. I kept quite still, for I was the Weakest and knew not what to believe.

In the Afternoon I heard a great Murmur of People in the innermost Courtyard, as the Carving was borne upon a Pushcart along the Street by the Executioner and placed in the Tower beneath my Cell. The next Morning around 9 the Carving was by the Executioner woefully mistreated, but gave out not a Sound. At the Time of the Midday Meal the Bailiff told the Woman how the Executioner had chopped off the Head of the Carving, had divided the Body into 4 Parts, each of Which was laid upon a Wheel and set up on the Gallows, and the Head was displayed before the Town Hall. The Bailiff stood in the outer Room and shouted this News loudly, that I should hear it, and repeated it three Times. I lay and thought over what I should do; I could not let it appear that I were not strongly affected by it, for at that some new Thing might be hit upon, to make me even more downcast ... I did not mind the Dishonour, for there were far too many Examples of great Lords in France, whose Images and Likenesses were burned by the Executioner, and who afterward again gained great Honour.

Of course it would have been worse if it had been her real husband who had been executed. But it would have been no less frightening.

For example, I've always felt that the most frightening thing about Don Juan as a figure, intended to inspire fear, is the fact that it's really a carving, a fiction, that is killed. It's not the real man who is condemned, the one who uses and abuses the earth and women in the name of progress and a perfect future. If it were, the judges would have had to condemn themselves and the pleasure they derived from law and order.

It's the fictive man who is condemned, the one who makes no progress at all, but clings to imbalances in the perfect moment. In that way the judges have clearly also judged themselves, but only by revealing their fear of chaos. And they are unanimous in advance about that fear, being above the law, just as the imperial elector is above the people.

This Don Juan enters the scene in 1630 in a peculiar blend of faithfulness and panic.

Tirso de Molina has chosen the perfect moment. Kepler dies, and his observations of sunspots are published. In Italy the plague is raging, with around two million total deaths. There are all kinds of reasons to devote oneself more or less cynically to the pleasures of the moment and dismiss fear.

The offense of the Don Juan figure is that he dismisses fear.

He transforms it to panic, as a last sign of his humanness.

Against all good judgment, he rises up from the flat earth and heads straight off into eternity.

In this singular and artistic way he indulges himself in cynical innocence.

He doesn't want to be human, he doesn't want to make progress, he wants to take on the vertigo and roll the whole sequence up into a pearl, no matter how distorted it becomes.

Don Juan has no use for reality. The less reality, the better. The only reality he accepts is his human body, which he cultivates to resemble forms belonging to the part of the universe that's entirely alien. The part that has never known, that has never been a body that could see.

Don Juan doesn't see reality. He doesn't see women. He sees only their shadows disappearing and making room for him and his body and his body's relationship to absolute panic. No one knows, after all, whether the universe is counting backward while we're so trustingly counting forward.

By humans he's condemned for his treatment of women.

By judges, for his lack of fear.

And by the gods, because he comes along carrying a carving and has left reality behind.

The freedom he demonstrates is not as much a rebellion against earthly order as an experiment with heavenly chaos.

The Baroque is this battle between the gods' right to fiction and humans' right to it. Who invented whom, and who is watching whom. "I think, therefore I am," wrote Descartes in that same century.

That sentence could easily have been more baroque: I think, therefore I am part of the labyrinth.

The labyrinth as a kind of shared thought process, a Möbius strip between humans and the world—and in that kind of labyrinth, it's actually only children who feel at home: for they break the spell by making it into reality.

(1978)

The Shadow of Truth

FIRST IMAGE. What I see might be a picture of a classical hero. A Greek athlete, a messenger. Night is falling in the mountains, maybe somewhere between Sparta and Athens, and the runner has sat down by the side of the road and unrolled his scroll. Maybe to check the route, the shortest way between his starting point and his goal, or maybe to check a message, but at any rate to orient himself a little better before it gets completely dark, and before he starts running again, which he will soon. As a hero on his way with a crucial communication. But isn't there something strangely stonelike about the sky? Isn't there something strangely like the sea bottom about the surface of the road under the scroll? And isn't there something strangely aquatic about the plants on the cliff? At any rate, it looks like some creature reminiscent of a jellyfish, a sea anemone, or a squid has taken shelter against the cliff for the night.

SECOND IMAGE. Is there a connection between the figure of the classical hero, the suggestion of a watery world, and the stone sky? At first I search the title of the picture for help. What I see has to be supplemented with what I don't see. Of course I still see the scroll with figures from Greek geometry, which, I am assuming, must be carried from one place to another. But now I'm forced to let what I see be guided by a name. Or more accurately, by two names. By the name "Newton," which is the title of the picture, and by the name Blake, the painter of the picture, who has made the picture symbolic by calling it "Newton." Because the hero has not only come running from Sparta to Athens, or vice versa, but he's also come running all the way up through the history of Europe, until 1795, when Blake placed him here on this roadside in the shape of Newton, a naked human figure who is no longer stopping to check the message and the route, no, he constitutes the message, he himself is the route that the message follows. For we all know that Newton, during a pause in the race, so to speak, changed our whole image of the world. But that change is connected with an image of the sky as wide-open space. Of the invisible ability of planets to move through something that looks like nothing. So why is Newton placed under a sky that looks like molten stone? Why is he sitting so rigidly against a cliff that looks like a volcanic reef? Hasn't he even noticed the squid, or whatever kind of sea creature it is that he's sharing the world with?

THIRD IMAGE. Now I'm looking for explanations further from the picture, in reference works. It's true that Blake's double exposure of Newton and the Greek athlete doesn't directly resemble New-ton, not the Newton I find in paintings done during his lifetime, where he's wearing a lace-trimmed shirt, a velvet jacket, and a long, curled wig. But I'll take Blake's word that this naked athlete doing calculations is the physicist, astronomer, and mathematician Isaac Newton, no less, Cambridge professor, Master of the Royal Mint, President of the Royal Society, discoverer of the law of gravity, the spectrum of visible light, and much more. I also find that Blake purposely made the illusion more believable by taking the drawing on the scroll from one of Newton's own books on optics. The hero as philosopher, as one who makes visible the workings of the world. When we add some speculation—the drawing on the scroll appears to be an equilateral triangle, which is a symbol of God, and inside the triangle an arc has been traced over the base, which might well be the geometric placement for all the points that we see from the base line beneath God's vantage point—then we're close to completely idealizing him: Newton as the naked, exposed human being who perceives the interrelatedness of everything. But moving on: Why is he exposed in this world of water and darkness? Why not in air and light? Why does he turn his back to all the glowing colors on the cliff and fix his gaze stiffly on the black-and-white figurative world of the scroll? I'm starting to think that I'm seeing him exposed at the farthest edge of a cliff that might well be triangular, as if he were in reality balancing, without knowing it, on the edge of the triangle that he thinks he has an overview of in the drawing. As if Newton were a victim of his own illusion.

FOURTH IMAGE. When I move even further afield, I find that early in Blake's artistic career he was already taking steps toward the Newton picture. In the early 1780s, Blake copied a print by Adamo Ghisi of one of the figures in Michaelangelo's frescoes in the Sistine Chapel: the Jewish king Abias, whom we know as the king who stood on a high cliff and exhorted his soldiers to go forth into the war he had inherited from his father, a war that he won. One doesn't see the whole story in Blake's picture; but one sees Abias portrayed with the same bent back and the same shield-like musculature as Newton, so that one could be tempted to say that Newton also inherited a war, and that he had to turn his back precipitously to the whole elaborate world in order to win that war. A second step appears in one of the pictures from Blake's series *There Is No Natural Religion*, a picture showing an old man kneeling on the earth, using a compass to draw an illustration over Blake's caption: "Application. He who sees the Infinite in all things sees God. He who sees the Ratio only, sees himself only." That is certainly also a war that's won, an insight that's found, and a humanity that maintains its courage because it has found the truth, in the form of Newton; but at the same moment that the truth is found, it shows its limits. For the truth that's been found is indeed true for all time, whether it has to do with Newton's laws or any of the other absolutes of science, but at the same moment that the truth comes to the light of day, errors come with it. Errors are, so to speak, the shadow of truth. The more all-encompassing the truth becomes, the more all-encompassing its shadow becomes. Because, as Blake notes somewhere, "All of us on earth are united in thought, for it is impossible to think without images of somewhat on earth." (Quoted in Northrop Frye, *Fearful Symmetry: A Study of William Blake*.)

FIFTH IMAGE. No one can see without a gaze that is, itself, part of what is being seen. So Blake's double image of the hero also becomes an image of the hero's shadow, of the luxuriant, manifold cliff that he's a part of, in the midst of the closed darkness of the sky, not realizing that the light he sees is a light coming from his own gaze. Placed in this shadow-filled counterimage, Newton comes to resemble Prometheus. Certainly Newton's heart, sex organs, and liver are there only in concealment, exactly in the center of the picture, to boot, so no eagle can rend his liver during the daytime, and no Zeus can regenerate it during the night. But it does seem as if he, in all his naked innocence, has stolen the gods' fire, and as if, as punishment for his careful observations, he is chained to the mountainside, exposed on the cliffs—not of the heart, but of the brain, inside his own skull, so to speak. An image of an immensely human powerlessness, where Newton's compass,with its tremendous wingspan, is transformed into the eagle that martyrs him. Day after day, the same touching attempt to pry the truth from life, to gain a depth of understanding that will reveal the whereabouts of God.

(1992)

The Shadow of Night

It's midnight, and without further ado we extend one day into another. Night after night we move into the same expansive borderland, where the forest up ahead is never really anything but the forest disappearing behind us, and where we barely manage to glimpse the white barrier at the frontier; it shows that it's 2400 hours on one side and 0000 hours on the other, before, in passing, we've transported the old day into the new one, so we never get a moment's rest, never a single second beyond the reach of time.

And why entertain the thought that time should stand still at exactly midnight? Like the thought that midnight on New Year's Eve stands even more still than on other nights. It's well known that time doesn't stand still. At least, not of its own accord. But with a little luck, time—the whole natural, mechanical, agreed upon human time frame—can be slipped into other time frames, so that from time to time we can experience what it would be like if time were to stand still. Not at any planned, prearranged point in time. More likely at the point when, on some occasion, we're so deeply immersed in the occasion itself that we forget time and place, forget ourselves, even completely forget the difference between ourselves and the world around us.

You might be standing still one night in a forest, in the same way that the trees are standing still. You lift your hand in the same way that the wind lifts a leaf. You listen to your own small sounds in the same way that you listen to those of your fellow creatures, you listen to your own breath as to the forest's. You have stepped into a different kind of time, a time with such slow turnings that you can feel in your very body that time is standing still. Never in your life have you experienced as many minutes as those in this forest time. But afterward, when you look at the clock, time—your own—has moved along as usual, in fact has flown, has vanished forever into that otherwise so inaccessible time that stands still.

So we actually have a very malleable relationship with time. We can move in and out of it as we like, can shorten or lengthen it to suit us. We can make it speed ahead, so that afterward we don't know at all where the time went, or we can make it trudge along, so that two little hours invariably feel like an eternity. We can do everything by the clock, or we can follow our own rhythms and only occasionally check to see what time it is. Basically we have two strategies: either keep an eye on time, or let time take care of itself. We combine these two strategies so that time keeps time with the wanderings of our consciousness in space. In that way, time itself becomes space, a long sequence of greater or smaller spaces, with life and events taking up more room than they otherwise would by purely chronological reckoning.

This shows that it's probably not time, the natural process we invented, that never lets us get a moment's rest. It willingly lets us step away from its numbers, to places where it's possible to view it all, if not entirely from the outside, then at least from places so mobile and changeable in relation to one another that a *web of time* arises, the illusion of an overview of the grid we've been caught up in. And that illusion becomes our little moments of rest.

So it's not time that we can't provisionally get beyond. More accurately, it's probably life. Life, our own, that never grants us a moment's rest. And thank goodness for that, we say time and again. But why can't we ever see what's beyond? Considering that we're constructed so that we're able to conceive of something beyond what we usually think of as beyond everything we know. Might it be because day and light can never really let go of us? Because we are children of light, as some hymn undoubtedly says? Simply because—more obviously than everything else—day begins in the middle of the night.

Or rather, day just keeps on going, on through the night, on through our dreams, where there's always enough light for us to see what's happening. And when we wake up, we have to concede that it's been day all night long, and that everything has kept going on its own. So night is just the beginning of day, as winter is the beginning of the year. And whether one is a bulb beneath the snow or a child in her bed, the light can always get in, as long as we live. And as long as we live, we can't think it away, either—the light.

Yet we can have a sense that in our thoughts, or in our sleep, now and then we brush against a different kind of night. A night that lies on the other side of the night we know. A night on the other side of all knowledge, of everything distinct and explainable, but also on the other side of what's unexplained, of what's uncertain, of fear and of all our illusions. A night that thinks us away, we might say, a bit aggrieved. At any rate a night without light, without differences, without any of the things we otherwise can name, a night defined by the absence of everything. And so it's quite possible for that everything to encompass its own absence.

Now, it's not only that day begins in the middle of the night; it's also that the week has seven days, but eight nights. So all the days are surrounded by nights. But even these surrounding nights aren't the original night: the night before the first night, and the night after the last night.

As the Greeks saw it, Night was the daughter of Chaos and mother of Sky and Earth. So the first night, the original night of the daughter of Chaos, has very little, maybe nothing in common with the normal earthly nights we know, which we might consider the civilized and enlightened children of a mother who, while just a child, the child of Chaos, was assigned the role of Night, the original blackness, about which we know nothing, and which we merely characterize on occasion, like Kazimir Malevich when he characterizes blackness as a square.

This blackness, this absolute night, is found at the boundaries of and beyond the reach of our senses. Black is certainly the sum of all the colors, but simultaneously it's the absence of color. To speak of something stripped, harsh, desolate, empty would be far too human, far too white and hopeful. This black is blacker. "Like a nothing without possibilities, like a dead nothingness after the death of the sun, without a future, without even the hope of a future, that is what it is like inside blackness," writes Kandinsky. And an artist ought to know.

Another artist, who may not have philosophized quite so much about blackness, but who certainly knew that the background of all paintings is absolute night, is René Magritte, who again and again painted the double game that nothingness plays with the most everyday objects, letting absence and presence enter labyrinthically into each other.

I'm looking now at one of Magritte's paintings. In the foreground the blackest black earth, from which a tree, vaguely poplar-like, rises like an elongated sphere. In the middle distance, a row of three-story, shuttered houses, which would be as black as the foreground if they weren't illuminated by an old-fashioned streetlight, just enough to let us see them as dark grayish blue-green structures that seem full of secrets. There are many sleeping secrets behind the closed shutters, and perhaps more disturbingly, waking secrets behind the last two windows, whose shutters still stand open. From those windows a golden light radiates, a light that could equally well be either sunrise or sunset. Behind the houses, another set of blackish bushes, like a berm along the sky.

The whole painting breathes night. Not without anxieties, this night and more night. Yet Magritte has called it *Empire of Light*. And of course he has a right to that and is right about that. For the sky over the darkened earth and its poplar-like tree, over the ghostly houses with their contrived lighting, the sky over this whole nightful arrangement is a bright summer sky, pale, with drifting clouds, maybe sixteen or seventeen nearly identical, fluffy classic clouds like those we know from the artists of the Renaissance. So night notwithstanding, there's daylight everywhere.

This is a scene Magritte has painted in various versions, with greater or lesser degrees of night darkness combined with light implicitly created by human beings, but always with this prototypical European summer sky overhead. He writes that in *Empire of Light* he has "merely reproduced certain occurrences, or rather produced a specific night landscape, as well as a sky like the one we see during the day. The landscape makes us think of night, and the sky of day. This simultaneous evocation of night and day seems to me to have the power to surprise and enchant. I call this power poetry."

An artistic concept, then. One that is perhaps right here at hand, because in the real world as well, it's true that the sky, especially at midsummer, can be surprisingly light-filled, over a landscape where it's already twilight; in fact even on a moonlit winter night, the sky can arch like a peerless cupola of light over dusky streets where darkness gathers and deepens.

But Magritte's sky is brighter even than the sky on a midsummer night. It's the sky of two o'clock in the afternoon, not two a.m., shining at its best. Magritte's sky is a constant. It's the brightest sky there is, and regardless of the time, it's populated with clouds whose shapes we fondly recognize and study. Magritte's sky is our own beloved summer sky, from when we as children lay on our backs in the grass, letting our thoughts roam, letting the clouds remind us of every conceivable thing between heaven and earth. The brightest of light, the endlessly open, but in Magritte's version, something that happens at night, in degrees of darkness and unspecified destruction. A true chiller of a night, where anything at all can happen and may well be happening. It's just that no one notices, because the sky is constantly, completely bright, keeping darkness and all the actions of darkness so constantly illuminated that they never can be evoked or seen.

Magritte titled his painting *Empire of Light*, a paradox, because he himself, like the viewer, must have been thinking of night. Because of this paradox—night and day experienced simultaneously—Magritte's paintings are generally labeled as surrealist, seldom anything else. But reality, from which surrealism arises and monitors its own foundation, does not disappear in that process. So when a daylight sky arches over an earthly, homestyle night, it may well clash a little with our senses, with the view we've come to consider the only one; but at night, between midnight and two a.m., when we close our eyes, we know perfectly well how natural it is for day to be right there with us.

We know perfectly well how familiarly we move through the day, but at night the day moves just as familiarly through us. At night, when we settle down so confidently in the shadow of the earth, we're confident only because we know it's the light on the other side of the earth that gives us our familiar place in the shadow. Light and shadow inextricably bound in our form of night, in which we rest within what never rests.

Basically we live in a kind of simultaneity of day and night. A simultaneity, or a poetry, that teaches us that we are immortal only as long as we're alive. Of course our nightly sleep, in the shelter of the earth's shadow, can be seen as practice for approaching absolute night. Between midnight and two a.m. we certainly think of death, without wanting to say so. Just as we think of war and know that it never will end until we bring enough of what we call night along with us during the day. How? Maybe we should always walk around casting a very long, oversized shadow on the sidewalk squares with every step we take, to remind us of nothingness. It's said that we waken from sleep at the moment when we dream that we're dreaming. Maybe we die at the moment when our shade becomes the shadow.

(1993)

The Seven Within the Die

God *is not dead*, I tell myself. God is the conversation that humans carry on with the universe, or vice versa: the conversation that the universe carries on with humans, in order to become conscious of itself.

I have to imagine (human that I am) that the universe wants to know something about itself.

I have to imagine that the chemistry of the universe has somehow stumbled onto itself and has singled out biology as a specific area for experiments, ones that include human consciousness. It's in this provisional biosphere that we walk around as the universe's guinea pigs. We know what we know, and to us it's priceless and vitally important, but I have to believe that ultimately it doesn't matter one iota, and that what this is really about is the chemistry of the universe actualizing itself as human consciousness in order to "know" itself.

I have to imagine that the universe is such a multifarious process that it couldn't avoid having blind, random chance draft the vision that's called humanity.

This humanity—its people and its societies, all expressed as biology—nevertheless seems to differ from biology, or nature, by gathering its many efforts and offerings and trying to put them all into play at once. As if we know that we'll only be in existence for a few seconds in the timescale of life's evolution over billions of years.

I have a calendar with an astonishing teaching tool, where four billion years of the planet's history are compressed into one calendar year. If the earth's crust hardens on January 1, then it's not until March 15 that the earliest stirrings of life begin slowly becoming bacteria and blue-green algae, and we have to get all the way to November 21 before animals emerge on land as mites and millipedes. On December 14 pterosaurs appear, and around Christmas, the first simians begin to climb trees. Not until the last day of the year, around 4:30 in the afternoon, do hominids of our own species begin fighting with other hominids. It's almost a quarter to midnight when we appear; it's five minutes to midnight when we create the first cave paintings, and it's one minute to midnight when we domesticate cattle. In this time frame, it's been forty seconds since Chinese pictograms were invented. Twelve seconds since beech trees first appeared in Denmark. Three seconds since we started wiping out other species.

It's inconceivable that this is happening, and it's inconceivable that we know this is happening. For me there's something enormously uplifting in the interplay between these two things that seem to mirror each other infinitely over a finite course of time.

It's the tension between what's inevitable and what's random, the juxtaposition of what I know and don't know—what I call thought— that decides my concept of reality. This, I imagine, is what allows the world to see what it's imagining.

It's these spiraling conclusions, and the way they never conclude, that make me think what I ultimately want to express is this: human beings have no choice but to imagine something more or less indefinite, as an expression of something definite that they can't imagine.

When I'm tossing a die that alternately rolls and stops, coming up as 1 or 2 or 3 or 4 or 5 or 6 in random order, I amuse myself by imagining the certainty that the die would never stop. Not on 1 or 6, or 2 or 5, or 3 or 4 ... I imagine it eternally rolling those opposing numbers around their impossible conjunction, deep within the center of the die, a three-dimensional seven in perpetual flux.

Why do I imagine things like that? Why do I keep playing with the thought that what's impossible must be possible? That the inconceivable should be conceivable? That random chance could be caught in its own trap? It has to do with being a tiny part of a humanity that has desperately denied its own randomness. Denied its own randomness to such a degree that it has tirelessly built up enormous, all-inclusive traps, calling them god, where it has held fast and preserved the restive prey of random chance, without wanting to understand that the prey is humanity itself.

No creature, no condition, no god can be held fast without dissolving. No consciousness, maybe no humanity, without being overtaken by other parts of the inconceivable process that keeps moving—not back and forth, but maybe in a kind of pulsation, corresponding to the interwoven, osmotic story the universe is telling itself in human beings' consciousness.

Merleau-Ponty writes so tenderly about the indescribable movements that must make up the dizzying underpinnings of what we, with growing hesitancy in recent centuries, have continued to call god, because "we have to conceive of a labyrinth of spontaneous steps which revive one another, sometimes cut across one another, and sometimes confirm one another—but across how many detours, and what tides of disorder!—and conceive of the whole undertaking as resting upon itself."

I can't help imagining labyrinths and more labyrinths within that very large and constantly moving labyrinth. A labyrinth for music, for instance. And a special little labyrinth-labyrinth for mathematics. And language as a labyrinth whose passages keep collapsing because words construct them only in passing, on their endless way toward the things whose shadows are buried somewhere behind them in the collapsed passageways. And that all these labyrinths breathe, open and close, turn and reflect themselves and each other, and allow all reflections to seep in and out, through each other, as the breath of the gestalt.

It's a story being told. About the simultaneity of everything in a discrete second. As when Novalis writes that "natural history must no longer be treated in discrete chapters for each subject—it must be (a continuum) a *story*, an organic growth—a tree—or an animal—or a human."

We have been removing things from their contexts for so long, and have altered nature's individual segments into arbitrary sequences, and are currently altering so many segments each day, that we have finally started to see that what we're altering is the whole.

We have finally started to see. Can we also understand and change and maybe learn to love our efforts again?

Can we borrow the optimism of Novalis, who writes, "We shall understand the world when we understand ourselves, because we and it are integral *halves*. We are God's children, divine seeds. One day we shall be what our Father is." Or, as he elaborates farther on, "God wants there to be gods."

Not everything is allowed, I tell myself. But if god didn't exist, then everything would, in principle, be allowed. The only exceptions would be the things that human society jointly agreed not to allow. But these things or laws are limited in advance by the workings of humanity. We mustn't kill each other—except during wars. We mustn't steal from each other—unless it's joy that we steal, or our fellow humans' self-worth.

If we pay people a wage that might seem high, for slaving like animals in slaughterhouses or other industries involving piecework, it's true that we're paying them for their efforts, replacing with money the time they have spent, but simultaneously we're stealing something irreplaceable, priceless: the quality of their working life, which is half of their entire self-concept as human beings.

If god existed, that kind of thing wouldn't be allowed. Not god as in religion, but god as in human tenderness toward all living things, including the air, the oceans, and the earth. Because all living creatures become earth and water and air when they die, so that the next living creatures can breathe and have enough food and water to form themselves into new life, maybe even new and better life.

A tenderness that applies not only to humans, but also to all the substances that humans are made of.

A tenderness that prohibits us from creating substances that threaten the substances humans are made of.

A tenderness that we can't afford to negate, not with money and not with arguments.

A tenderness that applies to everything, from the smallest things to the largest, and to all the parts' inconceivable, self-contained interconnections and balance.

Here humans are neither the smallest nor the largest, the best nor the most important; in the furthest reaching sense, they distinguish themselves from the rest of nature only by their ability to use the word *god*. By letting nature's many forms, including human forms of understanding, keep moving toward their shared incomprehensibility.

Living entities can be defined as things that come with projects, activities they want to carry out, because the activities want to be carried out in them.

In this way humans are creatures of myriad interpretations; it could be said that they come out in predetermined editions that remain unreadable along the way because they're not written until they've already been interpreted by consciousness.

This does not mean that humans can blindly follow their urges, their feelings, and their passions, and then excuse their actions by calling them fate.

Knowing something leaves us responsible for what we don't know. Making our lives readable leaves us responsible for what is in principle unreadable. Understanding certain parts of existence and of the world leaves us responsible for the myriad interpretations of the whole.

To me, these myriad interpretations are as crucial as they are difficult to live with. Almost every day, as I walk along the street, on the firm earth holding still beneath my feet, I have to convince myself, my whole body, that the earth is spinning.

When I board a train for somewhere far away, I often dream of an endless journey. I know I'm riding a train that runs on time, and

I'll arrive at my destination as scheduled, but I still indulge in the feeling of an ongoing endlessness, interrupted only when the train stops at, say, a station in a small town somewhere in Europe, where the fence is being painted as the stationmaster's wife putters in her rose garden, and I think that it could be me puttering there in the sunshine and warmth amid the fiery colors. Or I could be standing in an old coat in pouring rain, digging potatoes in a vegetable patch somewhere in Germany. Or sitting for hours in a railway station restaurant, while my consciousness continued its interrupted journey into another endlessness.

Somewhere Beckett writes, "Then I went back into the house and wrote: 'It is midnight. The rain is beating on the windows.' It was not midnight. It was not raining."

It's that simple to describe the first steps toward a life of dualities, the starting point for a life of myriad interpretations.

The problem is how to hold fast to a life of myriad interpretations inaccessible to our human systems, even though we're the most willing creators of systems in the world.

For the most part, we creep away from these myriad interpretations and their accompanying anxieties, creep into a more or less authoritative religion, a more or less obscure astrology, or a naive fascism, or else we put on superhero suits and try to plan things that have already happened, and call it politics.

Maybe that's the best we can do, when the facts we can convey to each other stay within the limited range of religious metaphors, or fascist advertising, or the equivocating language of political ideologies. To say nothing of the self-serving jargon of the sciences.

When we read declarations of human rights and similarly encouraging global agreements, they're good, and right, and hopeful, but one keeps wondering whether anything will come of them until we have the resources for them, given that most of the facts we exchange have to do with money and with control over specific materials (which actually belong to themselves and to the intrinsic balance).

Where will the energy and strength come from to create not happy conditions, but humane or natural ones on earth? Financing, wisdom, and justice are necessary components. They can bring about provisional progress in certain areas, they can be available for spontaneous revolutions and improvements in the balance of power, but they'll never be able to reveal that these improvements are a farce, because the ability to bring forth concepts of another kind of power lies beyond the scope of the language of financing, wisdom, and justice. We can't even bring ourselves to say that it's not humans who hold the power. Who would dare to say that for millennia now we've been fighting for a better distribution of power we don't even have?

I have to imagine that it's the earth that holds the power. I have to imagine that it brought its physical and chemical underpinnings into balance before it started creating what it continues to create, namely products that reproduce what has produced them, such as chestnut trees or human beings.

I have to imagine that humanity tends toward a shared imagery for expressing this power and its natural balances. That the individual person, left undisturbed, is a reflection of the condition of the earth, and that humans as a group are a chemical poem in praise of the earth and its sun.

We're becoming frightened now, when we see how nature is being ruined. But nature can still manage to heal our dreams; it will give us images and inspiration and lend joy and style to our love and our work.

We have not been sentenced to freedom, I tell myself. It's said we have been, because we haven't created ourselves and haven't had any part in deciding whether or not we're here; and it's said that we're sentenced to freedom because we alone, without god, bear responsibility for all our actions.

In keeping with this imagery, I experience us more as a group that has been reprieved, and that, through various lifetimes, moves about within an unmanageable prison.

Given our knowledge of the universe's chemical and electrical workings, it's a wonder that I'm not a stone, and it's pure chance that I'm not a mackerel having to reproduce somewhere beneath an oil-drilling platform in the North Sea.

In the circle game called "I Wonder," I'm "it." There I sit, like a little child, saying, "I'm a stone," or "I'm a fish swimming side by side with thousands of other fish." Even though everyone can see that I look like a human, am a human. But everything can be "I." That's our primary characteristic.

We can gather knowledge of stones, of fish, of ourselves. And we can make use of that knowledge.

With that knowledge we can actually deepen the sovereign knowledge we already have when we say "I'm a stone." "I'm a fish." "I'm a human."

I don't experience this "I" as something created. What I experience is the world, second by second, undertaking a division of its expressions, with the specific expression we humans call "the population of the earth" characterized by its millions of ways of saying "I," all with their foundations in a single way to say "god."

I don't experience this "I" as something whose presence I haven't had any part in deciding or defining. I don't experience myself as either definite or indefinite.

What I experience is that all that counts, by nature's reckoning, is whether we reproduce in the same way as jellyfish and ospreys and all the other phenomena that come slipping out of everything that already exists, grow, and become more numerous, and keep each other company for a while before we slip back again into everything that already exists.

What I experience is that the question of meaning and deciding can't be posed about existence. Existence is its own meaning. It's beyond discussion, because it is what is posing the question.

It poses the question by letting a part of its reproduction plan fit into the specific mental state called "I." It asks consciousness if it's possible, with the perpetually changing structures that have developed it (which human beings call "brains"), to achieve a complete reflection of the meaning that's already there.

I don't experience this "I" as something flung into freedom with an accompanying, enormous responsibility.

What I experience is that we have degrees of freedom of movement, expressed via style. In forms, also forms of relationship, where consciousness describes itself or its own structure.

I instinctively gravitate toward those forms. Like a bird building a nest in its natural environment. It's the beauty and truth in these forms that lets me feel responsible for my actions.

While chance does reign supreme, and I might just as easily have been a stone, a fish, or something else, what I can't escape is ultimately the something else that I might just as easily have been. It's not about freedom; it's about broadening our understanding of our connection to the other, to the other human or humans in the world. Its ultimate consequence has to do with broadening our responsibility to what seems an absurdity: that each and every one of us personally bears responsibility for every wrong action, even if it is committed by someone completely unknown to us.

This kind of thing is neither theory nor practice. It's magic. Or, to use a less loaded term, it's style. It has something to do with the following: Because humans use the word *god* (or have used it in the past), god exists (is still in existence) as the concept that corresponds to our sense of interrelatedness among all the atoms in the universe. (And so it's quite possible that *god* is a loaded word.)

I feel that what we call *style* is the closest we come to expressing that inconceivable concept. Style, with all its shifts in tempo, its areas of emphasis and its always surprising quantum ambiguities, which we find in music, for example, or in our social forms and their architectures.

The more or less overarching systems we build, which we call social order or universal order, have come into being as shields against the chaos that we believe is raging beyond what we've been able to organize and manage. Because we're afraid of death, of silence, and of darkness, yet also afraid of storms, volcanoes, and all sorts of earthly disturbances, we transfer our fear to our image of nature as a whole and place it in opposition to the human longing for order, cultivation, mastery, and development.

As a species we invariably adopt an arrogant attitude in our conversation with nature. The order we've imposed is the best, simply because it's our own, when in reality it's so poor that it can be maintained only because we ourselves have set up the caricature we're conversing with. But nature, the conversant whose expressible language is incorporated into us (as if we could play chess with ourselves without going insane), nature, which encompasses us and which we simultaneously encompass, is wholly an expression of the freedom that actually reigns supreme. Nature in itself bears no resemblance to the distortion resulting from what we, misguided by our fear and trembling, are trying to control.

Birds sing, springtime overwhelms us, hyenas devour carcasses, and the stars move along as if there were nothing to change. Star time is so enormously slow and has such extremes of tempo that there will have to be many more humanities before we comprehend the working processes of the universe as music. Bird space, especially songbird space, is so short and deep and inaccessibly lovely that we're delighted, but our pure delight, which I think relates to the electrochemical modulations of our biology, is drowned in our internal metronome, the heartbeat that binds our experience of tempo, weight, and value. Hyena space, which is close to the places where worms whisper and rustle about our bodies, spreads its near-inaudibilities, as if the haze over the savannas could be picked up as widespread sound, or as if the deepest processes of transformation, the processes of decay that await us, could be felt as carpets of sound, woven from time, spreading and vanishing.

Humans do not invent humans, I tell myself.

I do not believe that a particular freedom applies to humans. That's something we deceive ourselves about because we generally look at our lives as a series of private states of consciousness.

If I limit my view to the time that has passed in my life up to now, and, with my pulse rate as a fear meter, see death coming nearer, then I have to conceive of my life as an isolated travesty.

But if I experience, feel, my life as an example of something that stays alive no matter what, something that occasionally attains expression in me as in others, then I experience life as an anonymous drawing in which only the human characteristics shift.

If my child presses me, in all possible ways, to demonstrate my love and care, even though I may already be flooding him or her with love and care, then I take it primarily not as the child's desire to be in control and gain power, but rather as a need to confirm the reality of love in the world, from long before we met. Ego and love combined, because what is being expressed is a state of belonging, an interdependency in the world.

A world where it's not possible to invent oneself as a human, free and self-sufficient and pulled from thin air; it's possible only to follow and in that way illustrate the traces of humanness that we're drawn toward, in the truth that we're born into.

It's the same with what I've written here. To myself, as much as to anyone else. I write in the certainty that this has already been written before, in all possible ways, and that all its wild self-contradictions are a part of that reassuring form. It should have been a lullaby, like the one that waves write on water:

Humans are not abandoned and alone, it tells itself.

(1977)

Snow

It's snowing. I'm thinking back to January of 1979, when I received a letter whose writer told of his sudden fear of snow; for an instant the snow floating down to earth had been a poison that smothered all life.

It's snowing. I'm remembering the farmer on TV who told of walking out into his fields in early November, and the snow, the first very sparse and fine snow, burned like fire. But now, so much later, nobody would believe it. Even though practically every child knows that snow and fire are no longer opposites. Not in a radio-active world.

So. It's snowing. The snow is no longer snow, but it's still snowing.

We're now so fearful that we're not even fearful anymore, but the fear is spreading anyway, and the closest word for it is sorrow.

We see what's happening, and we're happy about what's not happening. We compare what's terrifying with what's even more terrifying. We compare limited nuclear war with total nuclear war, and the comparison deprives us of the last remnant of our natural horror.

We see thousands of dead birds, thousands of dead and maimed soldiers, thousands of death wishes and their violent expressions, but as long as we see all this annihilation in all its well-known forms, at least we're seeing something, and as long as we see something, total annihilation hasn't happened yet.

So fear has become a strangely useless feeling, discarded and purposeless, and over these chaotic fragments of a fear that once had a social purpose, sorrow has spread. The future is dead and buried, and the work of transforming ourselves from mourners to survivors, or at least to people capable of surviving, has barely begun.

At night we sit frozen to the TV screen, and night after night, the same thing happens: first President Reagan comes on and then General Haig comes on, and night after night Reagan says we're optimistic, and night after night Haig says that no one, and he means no one, has a monopoly on virtue.

No, we're not really afraid anymore.

It's true that we have a map of Denmark where someone has shown what will happen when, in due course, an atomic bomb falls on Copenhagen. What will happen is that Copenhagen will turn completely red, and the redness won't pale to gentle, pink radioactive fallout until way out in western Jutland.

But we don't react anymore. We don't pack any little brown suitcases with the things we'd need if we were trying to escape, and we don't pile up any sandbags, either, in the bedroom or by the front door. We see what's happening. We can't get alerts, and we don't want any. But occasionally, in the best Jules Verne fashion, in a dream of getting through all dangers, we set out and arrive safely at our destination, where we dig ourselves down into a mountain cave deep under the Siberian snows.

JANUARY 1982

It's snowing. It keeps on snowing. The radio broadcasts music and weather reports, music and weather reports, and the call goes out for all civilians to refrain from driving, making unnecessary telephone calls, or contributing to the chaos with their usual defiant attitude toward the weather gods, but to get themselves home, before the roads close, before one part of the country after another shuts down, and the whole country ends up paralyzed. At that point, military tractor-tread vehicles will be the only things capable of moving the immovable snow around, the only ones bringing food out to the stricken families, the only ones providing fodder for the radio's spirited accounts of birth and death in the drifting snow.

And meanwhile Haig appears on the screen. I've said before, he says, and I'll say again, he says, that no one has a monopoly on virtue. If the USSR thinks they have a monopoly on virtue, the USA knows how to break that monopoly. And that goes for every bit of virtue in the world: if it threatens our American direct and swift access to virtue, then the US has the power and the ability and the will to use its power to defend that virtue. Virtue is certainly not an inalienable commodity. It must be fought for and won again and again; this means that a great country certainly can lose its virtue, but not without fighting, for a great country can never lose its greatness or allow itself to lose face.

We talk about the commission that's been set up. It would be very good if we were less vulnerable, especially during snowstorms. It would be very good if we were less dependent on General Haig's attempt to make a virtue of necessity or vice versa. It would be very good if we were better at survival, on the day or night when, under cover of the first, the best, round of snow, we were invaded by Russian polar commandos, while all the Danish tractor-tread vehicles are on their way out to assist all the Danish motorists. All in all, it would be very good if there were a meaning to it all.

JANUARY 1983

It's snowing, but it doesn't matter.

General Haig is being interviewed by Secretary of State Haig, or vice versa, but it doesn't matter.

The neutron bomb has been put into production, but meanwhile we're using our time as wisely as we can; we insulate our life with a vengeance, shut out everything that can possibly be shut out, and give ourselves over to living in house slippers in the living room; and when the pot of potatoes is taken out of its haybox it coincides exactly with the beginning of "War Games in Denmark" on TV. "When the war comes, I'm going to hide in the haybox," says the youngest child. "It's so nice and warm in there."

The neutron bomb has been put into production, but there do seem to be plans to examine the civic bomb shelters. We're not sure if we'd need to bring water along.

I'm sitting here thinking about why it's only greed and fear that motivate us toward these sensible pursuits that, to put it bluntly, are sensible only because everything everywhere is so senseless. Why we don't use all our sense to establish peace, or use all our instincts to maintain life. Human beings' peace needn't be as different as we think it is from birds' peace; their musical division of the country — so that each individual can take care of itself and thus help to further the entire race — is all in all a better idea than our economic division.

But that's ludicrous; it's a false analogy; human beings aren't birds, and if they are, most of them are raptors.

But that's precisely the point. All human beings are actually sparrows, songbirds, siskins, parrots, and the like. They're prey to chance. And as prey, they aren't guaranteed a long and fruitful life, not without implementing a comprehensive warning system, a meticulous knowledge of the area, and a network of hiding places.

JANUARY 1984

It's snowing. Visibility is sharply reduced.

Whereas in earlier wars it was soldiers who died by the hundreds of thousands and civilians who mourned their deaths, it's now probable that if war breaks out it will be civilians who will die by the millions, with soldiers the ones left to mourn them.

How else could it be? Considering that the home front will either quickly dissolve or be directly wiped out, so that the soldiers will have nothing left to defend, then it will be the soldiers themselves who will have to try to survive at all costs, and to dig themselves down, as many as possible, into their underground command centers.

In any case, they have gas masks and radiation detectors, and they most likely have protective suits and food as well. I'm not sure if they thought about bringing water along. But of course they must have; maybe they even have machines that can melt the poisonous snow into something whose effect resembles that of water.

JANUARY 1985

It's snowing, and the snow obliterates all traces.

We steal around taking classes on securing everything and everyone against everything and everyone. Classes in defense against everyone and solidarity with everyone. Classes in obstruction, sabotage, and icy courtesy. As it snows, and the snow obliterates all traces. And as the atomic procession winds through a snow-covered Europe, we sit frozen in front of our TV screens and watch the snow keep snowing, obliterating all traces.

It's snowing; visibility is sharply reduced. We don't dare leave the TV off. Since the atomic bomb was dropped on the mountains of Iran, and since parliament voted to dissolve Denmark's ties to NATO (Haig in passing pushed the press aside and said it was impossible for NATO to pay attention to "a small country's one-sided decision"), and since the Strait of Hormuz was closed, since the oil stopped coming, since we started to get cold, we've kept the TV on. It gives off warmth, and at least it feels like an alarm system. As long as we can see an atomic bomb exploding on-screen, at least we know that we ourselves haven't been hit. As long as we still have hope that the gas masks we've saved up for will be delivered. As long as we can say that where there's life, there's hope. Maybe we can manage to figure something out. Because no one has a monopoly on death.

(1981)

The Miracle Play of Reality

I'm sitting here writing. (Language.) I'm writing this newspaper column and will receive money for it. (Work.) A column about my philosophy of life. (Feelings.) I (I), who once was born and immediately found myself among my fellow creatures (Humans), am sitting here writing in a Copenhagen apartment. Someone must have built it at some time (Social System). It has a history. A life span, one of many on the earth (Nature). Earth, which we can now see from space. There it hangs. That's where I live (Universe).

(The universe with nature with the social system with humans with me with my feelings, my work, my language, and more—all these and their mutual interrelationships are incorporated into my concept of the world, which is in constant flux, but on which I base everything anyway, as if it were what we call a philosophy of life— one that's a process, where seeing can't be separated from a life that both sees and can be seen, and that, when it expresses what it sees, demonstrates its innate inexpressibility.)

(The universe.) A wonder. That the sun, a roaring ball, destroying itself over the course of millions of years, creates life. For what we call eternity sunlight will arrive with exactly the delay needed to create life on earth and to maintain it. Not as eternal life for the individual. But eternal life for the integrated whole, in a kind of equilibrium between life and death. In terms of the whole, eternal. Until the sun burns out. So we live in a world where creation and destruction pulse as aspects of each other in vast natural surroundings. And we have to believe that, aside from the animals that see us, we are alone in our knowledge that we are here.

(Nature.) There too, wonder. Daily wonder. For example, when I watch the weather report on TV and learn not only what the weather will be like tomorrow, but also what the earth looks like right now. There it floats. Illuminated by the sun.

From a distance, so peaceful and lovely. The familiar shapes of the continents. The expanses of green, the blue of oceans. Here and there the glint of snow and the darker clusters of mountains, the branching rivers. Now and then wrapped in swirling clouds.

And up close, seen from human eye level, still peaceful and lovely. But simultaneously roiling and unlovely. Continuous repetition of forms and patterns. Comforting. But at the same time: unnerving progressions toward the catastrophic, toward stages of breakdown and decomposition. Unthinkable decay.

Case in point: the loveliness of everything we know about the natural world. The loveliness in the periodic table of the elements, for example, and in the mathematical attributes of plants and the symmetries of animals. But at the same time, the horror of what else we know. Of the doom of that loveliness, a downward spiral, uncontrollable and ruinous.

Placed in this precarious situation: the whole conglomeration of living creatures, including humans. Why are we here? In among all the nonhuman creatures, which simply exist. Beyond good and evil.

(The Social System.) Again wonder. The image of any one of the world's metropolises, seen from a plane gliding in for a landing: the city as a repetition of nature's patterns, a pulsating organism whose metabolic shifts between order and disorder are maintained by nature's most restless creators of social systems—namely us, humans, who, like ants, for example, move the world's materials around, but who, unlike ants with their meticulous consumption, seem to be transforming more and more of the rich and generous world of nature into an exclusively human world.

In this human world we don't leave scent tracks to regulate our shared behavior.

We are a part of nature, but at the same time we're the one part that can reflect on nature and in that way reflect on ourselves.

This duality—the fact that we not only are both evil and good, but also can see that we're both evil and good—is of course something special, but it wouldn't be worth anything at all if not accompanied by wonder, recognition, hope, compassion, love, forgiveness . . . by everything in us that's human.

In this humanness, we can't settle for letting things happen as they will, for being alternately evil or good, or both at once—and then assume that problems will work themselves out, if we're lucky.

Precisely because we can see that the forces of nature (also those within us) are beyond good and evil—because nature always does only what's possible—we must do the impossible. Not do away with evil, since we can't do away with part of our own nature, but love the good. Love.

That's why we can't just shout freedom, equality, brotherhood, and then think that evil has been done away with.

Being free and being bound, being equal and different from each other, living in brotherhood and being on our own are all sides of the same humanity.

This humanity is a process, an ongoing relationship. We have to be free, yet bound together as much as possible. We have to be equal, alike, yet as different from each other as possible. We have to be on our own, self-sufficient, yet share as much as possible.

The poverty that undoubtedly made socialism's narrow slogans necessary has been turned into prosperity, but it's a generalized prosperity, which doesn't include everyone; this means it's a prosperity that reveals that freedom, equality, and fraternity are only one side of the coin. The other side—being bound, also to our place in nature; having differences, diversity, which we also find in nature; and living our individual lives, which we borrow from nature—this other side can ensure that we don't trade freedom for greed, equality for envy, and brotherhood for sanctioned surveillance.

We do have a tendency to stay passive. "Whatever works," we say. As long as we agree and share equally, then we feel free to acquire as much of everything as we want and, just by labeling the earth's matter as "raw materials," to convert it into a man-made world. But it becomes a world with an entirely different kind of poverty. A world devoid of mercy.

(Humans.) So just what is the mercy in the world? Might it lie somewhere between wonder and forgiveness? We can see, hear, smell, taste, feel. We can move, eat, sleep, reproduce. And we can speak, dream, play, work. But can we also, by recognizing the miracle play of reality in one another, forgive and be forgiven?

Can the earth forgive us? The earth that, with its opportune relationship to the sun, took millions of years to create a foundation of nature where we, one completely arbitrary day in the timescale of the universe, could come into being? But we had been here for barely a few millennia before we put this foundation of nature in danger. The balance of creation and destruction as two aspects of the same thing—we're disrupting it. The whole nonhuman world, beyond good and evil, which we must both use and defend ourselves against—we're intervening in it, transforming it, changing its composition (also biologically), so that it's gradually becoming so much a man-made world that it's no longer beyond good and evil. It's becoming a play devoid of miracles, where the natural progression from destruction toward renewed creation is beginning to seem almost impossible. For example, in Chernobyl.

Can the people who live there—or more accurately, who now must live everywhere else except there—forgive. Can the people living in impoverished countries forgive. Can we forgive ourselves? I don't think forgiveness is something we can work to achieve. But I do think that work in itself can lead to forgiveness. Not work for the sake of money. But for the sake of our shared survival, along with work for its own sake. Not work to gain control over things and existence and the world, but work that's part of the process of creation that work itself provides insight into. And there is no work that doesn't do that, whether it's housecleaning, manufacturing, customer service, art, garbage collection, caring for others, or whatever it might be. Degrees of play—which always is deeply serious, when we devote ourselves to it.

(I.) I'm still sitting here writing. (Language.) I'm writing this newspaper column and will receive money for it. (Work.) A newspaper column about my philosophy of life. (Feelings.) "I" can step back a bit. I can let everything arbitrary, personal, everything that wants power over things recede a little within me, so things can come into their own. Love. I can act as if what I see, can see me. I can examine humanness by revealing it through my way of examining things. Poetry.

(1990)

"There is the landscape's time ..."

There is the landscape's time.
Hour after hour the landscape lies
watching us, dreaming up its own ideas,
usually in the form of grass. Now and then it puts
a humanity into the world, probably in hopes of being
able to speak. Then the marshes keep waiting, supplying
the willow thicket with water, and the flowers flock through one
century after another, and the mountains hold themselves up a little
longer. Surely you remember the landscape in a certain place on earth
in the morning, maybe on a Sunday, when the fish hung motionless in
the water, and the only sound was a single loud unanswered cry. In the
same way, one morning you're suddenly stopped by a flower that looks
at you searchingly. The whole surrounding landscape holds its breath.
But all you can do is long for rain. And so we keep being a random,
passing humanness, overcome by love and made mute. Then
the grass starts over. And the plants, which are God's affair.
The palm trees placed in the former factory building.
The wooden houses we can put on like coats. The
stones walking on like shoes. Infinitely slowly.
The landscape that heals all wounds.
Long after you are dead.

(1976)

Inger Christensen and I collaborated on the poster announcing my 1976 exhibition in Copenhagen. I gave Inger some drawings to write from, and she ended up with "There is the landscape's time …"

Inger wrote her text by hand on plastic foil, and I inserted parts of the drawings into the circle that we decided should be on the poster. I remember what a puzzle it was to compose all the circle's parts. In the printing office, drawings and text were transferred to a lithographic metal sheet and printed on brown deckle-edged paper.

—JOHANNE FOSS